INVITATION TO
THE NEW TESTAMENT EPISTLES I

This volume completes the ten-volume series of commentaries on the book of the New Testament, specially designed to answer the need for a lively, contemporary guide to the written Word. Here is the best of contemporary biblical scholarship, together with the world-renowned *Jerusalem Bible* text. In addition, there are study questions that will provoke and inspire further discussion.

The Pauline Epistles have traditionally been considered as letters from the great "Apostle to the Gentiles" to the churches he founded. In these letters to the church in Galatia and the church in Rome, Paul writes to fledgling communities beset by divisions of all kinds between the local churches and the authorities in Jerusalem. These epistles, long considered masterpieces of Paul's preaching, capture the power of the gospel, the passion of the Apostle, the uncompromising demand of faith, the struggle of living in community.

Just as he spoke to the Christians of his day, Paul speaks to today's followers of Christ. The problems he wrote about are still found in today's world and studying these epistles can be of help, solace and inspiration.

INVITATION TO THE NEW TESTAMENT EPISTLES I presents these epistles and their message in a format that can be easily used for individual study, daily meditation and/or group discussion. It is an indispensable volume for any Christian library.

INVITATION TO
THE NEW TESTAMENT EPISTLES I

INVITATION TO THE NEW TESTAMENT EPISTLES I

*A Commentary on Galatians and Romans
with Complete Text
from The Jerusalem Bible*

MARY ANN GETTY

IMAGE BOOKS
A Division of Doubleday & Company, Inc.
Garden City, New York
1982

The texts of the Epistles to the Galatians and to the Romans are from *The Jerusalem Bible,* copyright © 1966 by Darton, Longman & Todd, Ltd., and Doubleday & Company, Inc. Used by permission of the publisher.

Library of Congress Cataloging in Publication Data

Getty, Mary Ann.
  Invitation to the New Testament Epistles, I.

  (Doubleday New Testament commentary series)
  Bibliography
  1. Bible. N.T. Galatians—Commentaries. 2. Bible.
N.T. Romans—Commentaries. I. Bible. N.T. Galatians.
English. Jerusalem Bible. 1981. II. Bible. N.T.
Romans. English. Jerusalem Bible. 1981. III. Title.
IV. Series.
BS2685.3.G47   227'.1077

Library of Congress Catalog Card Number: 79-6585
ISBN: 0-385-14796-1   AACR2

Commentary Copyright © 1982 by Mary Ann Getty
General Introduction Copyright © 1977 by Robert J. Karris
All Rights Reserved
Printed in the United States of America
First Edition

To Bill and Nina, my parents.
You have given me life and a
heart filled with gratitude.

CONTENTS

GENERAL INTRODUCTION	15
INTRODUCTION	19
THE LETTER OF PAUL TO THE CHURCH IN GALATIA	33
THE LETTER OF PAUL TO THE CHURCH IN ROME	115
SUGGESTED FURTHER READINGS	283

ABBREVIATIONS OF THE BOOKS OF THE BIBLE

Ac	Acts	Lk	Luke
Am	Amos	Lm	Lamentations
Ba	Baruch	Lv	Leviticus
1 Ch	1 Chronicles	1 M	1 Maccabees
2 Ch	2 Chronicles	2 M	2 Maccabees
1 Co	1 Corinthians	Mi	Micah
2 Co	2 Corinthians	Mk	Mark
Col	Colossians	Ml	Malachi
Dn	Daniel	Mt	Matthew
Dt	Deuteronomy	Na	Nahum
Ep	Ephesians	Nb	Numbers
Est	Esther	Ne	Nehemiah
Ex	Exodus	Ob	Obadiah
Ezk	Ezekiel	1 P	1 Peter
Ezr	Ezra	2 P	2 Peter
Ga	Galatians	Ph	Philippians
Gn	Genesis	Phm	Philemon
Hab	Habakkuk	Pr	Proverbs
Heb	Hebrews	Ps	Psalms
Hg	Haggai	Qo	Ecclesiastes
Ho	Hosea	Rm	Romans
Is	Isaiah	Rt	Ruth
Jb	Job	Rv	Revelation
Jdt	Judith	1 S	1 Samuel
Jg	Judges	2 S	2 Samuel
Jl	Joel	Sg	Song of Songs
Jm	James	Si	Ecclesiasticus
Jn	John	Tb	Tobit
1 Jn	1 John	1 Th	1 Thessalonians
2 Jn	2 John	2 Th	2 Thessalonians
3 Jn	3 John	1 Tm	1 Timothy
Jon	Jonah	2 Tm	2 Timothy
Jos	Joshua	Tt	Titus
Jr	Jeremiah	Ws	Wisdom
Jude	Jude	Zc	Zechariah
1 K	1 Kings	Zp	Zephaniah
2 K	2 Kings		

GENERAL INTRODUCTION TO THE DOUBLEDAY NEW TESTAMENT COMMENTARY SERIES

Let me introduce this new commentary series on the New Testament by sharing some experiences. In my job as New Testament Book Review Editor for the *Catholic Biblical Quarterly,* scores of books pass through my hands each year. As I evaluate these books and send them out to reviewers, I cannot help but think that so little of this scholarly research will make its way into the hands of the educated lay person.

In talking at biblical institutes and to charismatic and lay study groups, I find an almost unquenchable thirst for the Word of God. People want to learn more; they want to study. But when they ask me to recommend commentaries on the New Testament, I'm stumped. What commentaries can I put into their hands, commentaries that do not have the technical jargon of scholars and that really communicate to the educated laity?

The goal of this popular commentary series is to make the best of contemporary scholarship available to the educated lay person in a highly readable and understandable way. The commentaries avoid footnotes and other scholarly apparatus. They are short and sweet. The authors make their points in a clear way and don't fatigue their readers with unnecessary detail.

Another outstanding feature of this commentary series is that it is based on *The Jerusalem Bible* translation, which is serialized with the commentary. This lively and easily understandable translation has received rave reviews from millions of readers. It is the interstate of translations and avoids the stoplights of local-road translations.

A signal feature of the commentaries on the Gospels is that they explore the way each evangelist used the sayings and deeds of Jesus to meet the needs of his church. The commentators answer the question: How did each evangelist guide, challenge, teach and console the members of his community with the message of Jesus? The commentators are not interested in the evangelist's message for its own sake, but explain that message with one eye on present application.

This last-mentioned feature goes hand and glove with the innovative feature of appending Study Questions to the explanations of individual passages. By means of these Study Questions the commentator moves from an explanation of the message of the evangelist to a consideration of how this message might apply to believers today.

Each commentator has two highly important qualifications: scholarly expertise and the proven ability to communicate the results of solid scholarship to the people of God.

I am confident that this new commentary series will meet a real need as it helps people to unlock a door to the storehouse of God's Word where they will find food for life.

ROBERT J. KARRIS, O.F.M.
Associate Professor of New Testament Studies
Catholic Theological Union and
Chicago Cluster of Theological Schools

INTRODUCTION

It is a continually fresh source of surprise that someone like Paul, who wrote letters almost two thousand years ago, still intrigues and challenges us today. This man, who did not even seem to fit into the culture and religion of his own times and still seems abrasive to ours, has nevertheless irrevocably touched our lives. Try as we might, we cannot avoid the challenge that Paul holds out. The mystery of it all is that the more we try to sound the depths of Paul, the more we are impressed with his elusive, impossible-to-contain appeal. In him we recognize a pastor immersed in his preaching task, totally involved in the church of his day. The arena where he shaped his message could seem circumscribed by our own global standards. The problems he addressed could seem outmoded for us. We might sense in ourselves some nostalgia for the apparent simplicity of his times—for the fact that he freely dispenses advice to a church less complex and fettered than the church today. And his recommendations about which foods can be eaten (e.g., Rm 14:1–6, 14–15, 20–21), whether pagan converts should be subject to the law (e.g., Ga 2:15–3:5, 5:1–12), or whether Christians should pay taxes (e.g., Rm

13:6–7) could seem like easy solutions but hardly applicable to today's complex church and world problems.

Yet this does not at all reflect our real experience with Paul. He cannot really be dismissed, no matter how cavalierly we try to tailor our attitude against him. His very tenacity as a model of a Christian preacher haunts us, and somehow, however reluctantly or warily, we are drawn back to him again and again. We cannot ignore even a letter like Philemon—a short, dated letter addressed to an individual and dealing with the problem, nearly obsolete today, of slavery, a problem that we would like to protest that we have long since overcome. But Philemon returns with its challenge that gnaws at complacency and continues to raise the question of how practical and real one's commitment to Christ is. Even less can we ignore the implications of the message of Galatians and Romans, two epistles long recognized as masterpieces of Paul's preaching. These epistles capture the power of the gospel, the passion of the Apostle, the uncompromising demand of faith, the struggle of fleshing out its truth in community. No matter what we instinctively feel for Paul, the immensity of the debt Christianity owes him forces us to accept that his words are here to stay and they continue to attract and nourish us as Christians. We take them as gospel.

It is important to remember that Paul is the first Christian writer. The Gospels as we know them did not yet exist when Paul took up his pen. He develops "the gospel" before the evangelists Matthew, Mark, Luke and John began to write. Paul calls himself an "apostle" before a written account of Jesus' earthly life with his disciples existed. We are used to thinking of the Gospels as the four narratives that chronicle Jesus' ministry of word and deed in Israel until his death at the hands of the Romans and Jewish leaders. The four Gospel accounts describe in different detail the impact of Jesus' earthly ministry on the various people he encountered—on his disciples and the Twelve, on his friends and opponents, the Jewish leaders, on women and on the poor. There is a story line developed by the Gospel writers who follow Jesus from his early life and ministry to his death and Resurrection. These four accounts, written for four different audiences, reflect the primitive Christian communities' struggles with questions of christology, liturgy, morality, faith. They portray Jesus relating to his world, speaking in parables, healing the sick, admonishing the leaders, praising the children.

Paul's gospel is different, model though it is. Insofar as he can define it, Paul calls the gospel the power (the Greek word is *dynamis*) of God. Paul hardly ever refers to the earthly life of Jesus or to any of its events. For Paul the Resurrection is faith's focus and the gospel means universal salvation. Paul was inspired to write because of preoccupations similar to those of the evangelists—questions of christology and the threat of any piety that would canonize intellectual assent or ritual legalism without properly emphasizing community and ethics. Like the evangelists, Paul had to address questions that Jesus never answered. However slowly and gradually, the church was beginning to come to terms with the fact that Jesus' return was not going to be as soon as was originally expected, so that, in the meantime, many problems had to be resolved. The fledgling church was beset with internal and external difficulties. There were divisions within local communities, competition, prejudice and lack of mutual acceptance between local churches and the authorities in Jerusalem. There were problems of communication and consistency, aggravated by the confusing influences of false teachers and even by the vacillating of such church stalwarts as Cephas (Peter) himself (Ga 2:14; see comments below on Ga 2:1–10 regarding Paul's use—with one exception—of "Cephas" instead of the more familiar "Peter"). The gospel was to create community, but some interpreters wreaked the havoc of dissension. Paul's own authority was undermined by the agitators in Galatia, yet, in order to reassert the authority of the gospel, he forcefully refers to Cephas' weakening under pressure.

It becomes more and more evident that, whatever we do, we cannot take Paul lightly. He is too complex and too important. Much of Paul's complexity is due to his rich background and education that reflects his times. He was a Jew, trained as a Pharisee, educated in the finest Jewish circles, filled with zeal for the law to the point of being a fanatical persecutor of Christianity which he correctly perceived as threatening to the law. Paul was a Roman citizen, with all the rights and privileges of that status. Paul had the best education of the Greek world in which he was born and in which he was capable of challenging debate. The complexity of his polished education alone, however, does not account for the perennial interest in and importance of Paul for us. It was because Paul was seized by the gospel, transformed by its vision, converted from Judaism, and was a missionary to the pagans that Paul continues to represent our hope as Christians. He simply cannot be ignored.

Ever since he wrote them, his words have been met with anger, consolation, admiration, rejection, sympathy, denunciation, but never indifference. He has been labeled arrogant, egotistical, a crowd pleaser, an anarchist, a chauvinist, a legalist and a libertarian. He has been accused of everything from impossible idealism to crass realism, but never of mediocrity. He has also been called a saint, the architect and spokesman of Christianity. He who apparently never saw, walked or talked with the earthly Jesus has been associated with Peter as the proto-apostles.

It would be impossible to summarize the life and teachings of Paul, or even just of the development of Galatians and Romans in this brief introduction. This book at best can only begin to scratch the surface of a few of Paul's thoughts as they have been integrated in my own experience as just one student of Paul reflecting on years of exchange with other students of Paul. Aware of my own limitations, I shall confine my presentation of this great lover of God and people to three influences of his own experience that shaped, at least partially, his letters to the Galatians and to the Romans. These experiences are his apostleship, his vision, and what I call his principle of "universal inclusivism."

First, Paul was an "apostle." It was he who

shaped this term and then contributed it to the Christian heritage to be further developed by others. He borrowed it from his beloved Judaism which conceived the idea that an apostle, as "one sent," in a significant way represented the authority of the sender. Paul not only claimed this term for himself, but defended it vigorously, even against the other Apostles. Paul was an apostle to the pagans, and that made all the difference. The zeal that would carry him to the ends of the known world would not, however, ease the ache of his great heart for his fellow Israelites. When he went out to set the pagans free, he did not shut the door on the Jews. The super power he received from his call to preach the Good News among the pagans only heightened his feelings of powerlessness to remove the blindness of his own people. Paul's own personal conversion was at the same time his mission. He was not capable of separating piety from liturgy, community from ministry, personal sanctity from evangelization. When Paul heard God's Word, he was transformed from a fanatical Pharisee to an apostle consumed with hunger and thirst for justice to be available to the pagans. This zeal for the pagan mission did nothing to qualify or downgrade the importance he attributed to the Jewish mission. In fact, he pursued the mission to the pagans so relentlessly precisely because he began to see it as tied up with the mission to the Jews, as an essential stepping-stone to the conversion of the Jews.

Secondly, Paul was a visionary. Though many would dispute the meaning of Paul's visions, none has denied that he surely had them. Simple observation told the story that Paul the Pharisee-turned-Apostle saw things differently from one moment to the next. He was transformed from persecutor of the Christians to proclaimer of Christ. We have Paul's word that this was because he received a revelation (or apocalypse; Ga 1:12, 2:2) that changed the way he saw things and gave him amazing power to bring into a situation a dimension of insight that had not been there before. Where there was suffering, Paul saw hope. Where there was community threatened by outsiders and torn apart by internal divisions, Paul saw a unique opportunity to testify to the spirit of love at work. Where there was rejection of the gospel by the Jews, Paul saw the providence of God bringing the Jews to humbly accept the conversion of the pagans. Where there was tension between Jews and pagans, Paul saw the mystery of God unfolding. He broke into hymns of praise and thanksgiving that seemed to express Jesus' own wonderment that God kept such secrets from the proud and revealed them to children (Lk 10:21–22).

Thirdly, Paul was a universalist, or, to coin a phrase, a "universal inclusivist." Paul's apostolic vision rested on the conviction that God was revealing in the gospel the power save *all*. Paul's mission to the pagans signifies not merely a concern for a particular group (that is, non-Jews). Rather, the pagans represent the *universality* of salvation. All of the disenfranchised (i.e., the blind, the lame, the deaf, prisoners, women, the poor and other outcasts, foreigners, people of all nations) were collectively signified in the mission to the pagans. Circumcision, limited to men, was the rite of initiation into Judaism. To the Jews, it represented Judaism's exclusive claim to be God's people. It signified, for the Jews, God's choice of them rather than any other nation. A sign of the covenant, circumcision separated the righteous Jews from others. For the Christians and under Paul's influence, circumcision became the symbol around which swirled the question of the gospel's limits. How far from Jewish exclusivity could the gospel be taken without corrupting its message? How do we qualify, make manageable or even acceptable, the mandate to be the gospel's witnesses to the "ends of the earth" (Ac 1:8)? Even if sinners were circumcised, the Judaism of Jesus' day taught, certain of them were to be treated as uncircumcised and therefore outside the pale of salvation. Paul raises questions about what exceptions could be legitimate. If some could be circumcised and still not be saved and if others could be saved without circumcision, as the Jews themselves believed, then circumcision is not the real boundary between the saved and the unsaved. Paul maintains that, for the Christian, Baptism eliminates this distinction, and with it, any other distinction. The only requirement for Baptism is faith and faith is accessible to all. It is significant in this regard that Baptism for everyone, even for women, for slaves, for non-Jews, for foreigners and sinners, has from the beginning been the distinguishing mark of the Christian. Thus Baptism stands as a powerful symbol of the absolute inclusivity of the gospel. There is no principle that Paul defends so ardently, so consistently and so completely as the principle that the gospel includes *all*. Even if questions do arise in isolated communities about the role of women in the liturgy (1 Co 11:2–16, 14:34–35), even if Paul himself circumcises certain pagans (Ac 16:2–3) or even if he seems to condone the practice of slavery (Ep 6:5–9; Col 3:22–24), the inclusive, universalist message of the gospel is that salvation is for all, that "in Christ there is neither male nor female, Jew nor pagan, slave nor free, all are one" (Ga 3:28).

As an apostle, as a visionary, as a "universal inclusivist," Paul's total devotion is to Christ. And Paul makes this commitment real. That is, he really fleshes out his commitment to Christ by drawing out the implications of the love command that sums up all the law and the prophets, all of Paul's own teaching, "You must love your neighbor as yourself" (Lv 19:18; Rm 13:9; Ga 5:14).

GALATIANS AND ROMANS

The Epistle to the Galatians relates to the Epistle to the Romans, it has been said, as the rough draft does to the finished product. In general, Paul enjoyed more leisure and achieved greater objectivity in composing the latter epistle. There he developed his topics to greater length and with greater nuances. To the communities in Galatia, however, where agitators were stirring up the young church with ideas about the role of the law in incipient Christianity, Paul fired off an aggressive, no-time-for-nonsense letter that categorically denied the agitators' position and condemned the agitators themselves.

From the point of view of content, points of congruence between Galatians and Romans include the universality of justification apart from the law, the temporary and relative role of the law, the example of Abraham, the centrality of the love command, the spirit-flesh antithesis, the new creation of the children of God. The basic structure of both epistles includes roughly the doctrinal-theological foundations supported by Old Testament references, followed by the ethical exhortations, or what is called the "paraenetic conclusions." This structure is referred to as Paul's "indicative-imperative" pattern. In other words, he describes the new reality of justification by faith as the way things *are,* and only then does he draw ethical conclusions for the way Christians *should,* therefore, be and act.

But the differences between Galatians and Romans are also undeniably noticeable. The angry, emotional, brusque, pragmatic tone of Galatians betrays a writer frantically battling a declared and identified enemy. The disturbers in Galatia had threatened Paul's gospel and undermined his authority and the confidence in him of the communities there. So upset was Paul that he begins his letter without the characteristic prayer of thanksgiving. This absence indicates the all-or-nothing stakes that Paul knows are involved as he tries to convince the Galatians of the seriousness of the danger that threatens them. Romans, on the other hand, lays out, in the most systematic way available to Paul's mind, the gospel program. Paul assumes the position of one standing at the crossroads, surveying the horizons for the journey that lies ahead and looking back at the road already taken. Romans is like a guide written by a seasoned traveler who shares with a novice the wisdom of his experience. Paul, in Romans, can be emphatic, passionate, involved. At the same time, he has the advantage of a certain distance, for he has not founded the Roman community and it does not seem to be directly threatened. He enjoys a certain neutrality, for though he surmises the probable difficulties that a mixed community of Jews and pagans could encounter, he seems to be confident that they will be successfully resolved. He writes, too, with a certain vested interest, for he wants to visit Rome on his way to Spain, and so he carefully outlines his gospel in the hope that it will be accepted by the Romans and ultimately by all.

Galatians and Romans fit well together. They together fill out a portrait of their author since they reveal some of Paul's many sides as he addresses comparable communities, raising similar issues, from different, complementary, perspectives. As we undertake a study of these two works, our appreciation for this Apostle can begin to grow. He dares to express all the conviction, ardor, affection, commitment, fear and flexibility of a flesh-and-blood person with a mission to spread the Good News of salvation as far as he could. The key to his success, it seems, was in his deep awareness that it was the gospel experience which bound him to the Galatians and the Romans. And our key to understanding Paul is in the personal conviction that the same gospel binds us to him and to one another.

ACKNOWLEDGMENTS

We tend to see some achievements as milestones in our personal journeys. The completion of this book represents one such for me. I want to thank the publisher and editors, especially Robert Karris, O.F.M., for being so helpful and kind. I am indebted to my students for all they teach me. I am grateful to my brothers and sisters who are also my friends. And, of course, Romans would not be complete without Phoebe and all the goodness she represents.

MARY ANN GETTY, R.S.M.
Carlow College
Pittsburgh, Pennsylvania

INVITATION TO
THE NEW TESTAMENT EPISTLES I

The Letter of Paul to the Church in Galatia

Paul's Epistle to the Galatians has ranked, with the two letters to the Corinthians and that to the Romans, as one of Paul's four most important. There is no real consensus among scholars about Galatians' chronological relationship to Paul's other epistles, especially the complicated history of his correspondence with the Corinthians. Nevertheless, it is generally agreed that Galatians was written toward the end of Paul's writing career, about A.D. 55 or 56, a short time before the composition of Romans.

A unique feature of Galatians is that it was addressed not to one church of one town or city, but to the "churches" (1:1) of the whole territory of Galatia, in Asia Minor. (Note that the title "To the Church in Galatia" is employed by the editors of *The Jerusalem Bible,* but this is at variance with Paul's own words which address the "churches," in the plural.) It is uncertain exactly where the boundaries of Galatia were or how much of an area Paul had in mind when he wrote this letter to these communities. But the exact limits of the territory he envisioned are not essential to understanding his message.

Another aspect of this letter that continues to intrigue its interpreters is the precise origin and purpose of those who are disturbing the Galatian Christians, a community composed predominantly of converts from paganism. From what Paul himself says, it seems that agitators followed him around, alleging that the gospel meant that at least parts of Jewish law (3:1–3), including what pertained to circumcision (5:7–12), must supplement faith in Christ. The agitators suggested that Paul's evangelization was hurried and inadequate, that the Apostle had short-changed the Galatians in presenting them with a law-free gospel. Thus they undermined Paul's authority and the Galatians' confidence in him. The agitators claimed that they could rectify Paul's preaching by adding the law of Moses to the gospel Paul preached. Paul's reply by letter to the Galatians is no meek self-justification nor an apologetic defense of the gospel. He clearly points out that he was called by God and bears the authority of God (1:6–2:21). Then he challenges the preaching of the agitators while he chides the impressionable, easily led Galatians (3:1–6:10).

The epistle's structure is not complex. The short address and greeting without the usual thanksgiving (1:1–5) are followed by the doctrinal (1:6–4:31) and then the exhortatory ethical (5:1–6:10) sections and a brief conclusion (6:11–18). Among his doctrinal considerations Paul includes a description of his own call and mission and a challenge to any questioners or opponents (1:6–2:14). Next, he punctuates his development of the role of the law with personal pleas for the Galatians to remember his own example and experience with them (2:15–3:9). Typically, Paul strengthens doctrinal sections by giving Old Testament examples to substantiate his points (3:10–4:31). The ethical considerations follow in 5:1–6:10. There Paul exhorts the Galatians to live in freedom and love of one another. With 6:11–18, Paul closes the letter almost as abruptly as he began it. He writes these final verses in his own hand for emphasis, he reports (6:11), implying that the rest of the letter was dictated to a secretary or scribe.

Galatians 1:1–5
THE ADDRESS UNADORNED

¹ ² 1 From Paul to the churches of Galatia, and from all the brothers who are here with me, an apostle who does not owe his authority to men or his appointment to any human being but who has been appointed by Jesus Christ and by God the Father who raised Jesus from ³ the dead. ·We wish you the grace and peace of God our Father and of the Lord Jesus Christ, ⁴ who in order to rescue us from this present wicked world sacrificed himself for our sins, in accordance with the will of God our Father, ⁵ to whom be glory for ever and ever. Amen.

✠

Whereas it is modern custom to *close* letters with signatures, Paul *begins* his epistles by identifying himself. His identity means so much more than a personal handle or initialing. Paul's name means "small." It was changed (Ac 13:10) from Saul. In the long biblical tradition that colored Paul's self-description, a name change is extremely important; it signifies a new vocation, a new meaning in life. Similarly, in the Old Testament, Jacob's name was changed to Israel (Gn 32:29, 35:10), and in the New Testament, Simon becomes Peter (Mt 16:18; Mk 3:16; Lk 6:14; cf. Jn 1:42). After a Godly vision, a person's life takes a decidedly different direction. It is new life in God.

In Galatians, Paul describes his vocation as a divine call that even precedes his birth (Ga 1:15). He draws on the great prophets to describe his designation for a divine mission (Jr 1:5; Is 6:1-9). Yet in this Paul finds no cause for pretense, no ground for conceit. Paul distinguishes himself from the pillars of the church (Ga 2:9), the authorities, the more *likely* candidates for discipleship.

The term "apostle" by which Paul further identifies himself was coined by him rather than by the Gospel writers. This is a term that has certainly left its mark on the Christian tradition. Although "apostle" is frequently related to the Twelve, that is, to the inner circle of disciples who followed and served with Jesus during his earthly ministry and who in the New Testament represented the twelve tribes of Israel, the real theological significance of this term is traced to Paul whose letters preceded the Gospel writings. "Apostle" means "sent." With Paul's vocation (call), there is a mission (a sending). The term "apostle," a title Paul staunchly defends for himself, signifies unquestionable authority, the authority of God. In carrying out his vocation, Paul is representing not Cephas nor any other merely human disciple, but Jesus himself (1:15-16).

It is a unique characteristic of Paul's Epistle to the Galatians that it lacks an opening thanksgiving such as appears in Paul's other epistles (e.g., Rm 1:8; 1 Co 1:4-9). The Apostle's abrupt, businesslike beginning could therefore suggest that Paul felt he had little to be thankful for regarding the Galatians. But it is urgency rather than ingratitude that prompts Paul to hurry, as it were, to the core of his message. A formal thanksgiving would, of course, have required only a few words. But these few words might have distracted either his readers or Paul himself or both into a kind of complacent self-congratulation. Never does Paul seem to be more single-minded and less able to be distracted than in this letter. His tone is crisp, clipped, even biting. His focus is clear. As Apostle, he is entrusted with the message, authority, appointment of God. He is indebted to no one. He has no interest in the views or opinions of others regarding himself personally or his gospel. But he is concerned that others accept the truth. His apostolic heart cautions him that the gospel itself is being falsified when it is presented as a "first step" that must then be supplemented by the law.

Paul counters this distortion of his message strenuously, relentlessly. In no uncertain terms he insists on the divine origin not only of his personal authority but of the gospel he preaches. By the end of the epistle, readers have ample examples of the inseparability of Paul's authority and his gospel. In the process he spares nothing and no one. There is no holding back. The matters he needs to discuss, in response to the disturbances in Galatia, are too important to gloss over with the usual amenities. He is on the attack. Or, better, he is quick to the defense of his gospel under threat. He recognizes that the addition of the law to his gospel of Christ is a subtraction from grace which cannot be tolerated.

GALATIANS 1:1–5

STUDY QUESTIONS: How does Paul identify himself? What is the origin of his confidence as an apostle? Does he strike you as arrogant? Why? If Paul was appointed by Jesus Christ and by God, what is his greatest obligation?

Galatians 1:6 – 4:31
SETTING THE RECORD STRAIGHT

Paul now begins the doctrinal part of this epistle (1:6–4:31). Here he lays down the theological foundations for the exhortations (5:1–6:10) to the churches of Galatia. Paul's "doctrine" includes a review of his own authority as given by God (1:6–24) and approved by the church (2:1–21), followed by some conclusions about the temporary role of the law (3:1–9), which are substantiated by an appeal to the law itself (3:10–4:31).

Throughout his reflections on the theological foundations and implications of the gospel, Paul intersperses the testimony of his own experience. His call, his confrontation with church authorities, his defense of the pagan mission, his conclusions about the law's temporary and now superseded role, his antithetical reading of the Old Testament which later led him to oppose the law to faith—all of these are integral parts of Paul's gospel.

In the first place, Paul insists, the gospel is from God and no one can rescind it in whole or in part (1:6–10). It requires no supplement or abridgment, no commentary, approval, rationale. It just is. The gospel includes Paul's undeserved call and unqualified mission (1:11–24). From a human standpoint, Paul's past record effectively eliminated him from consideration as a candidate for apostleship.

But the divine origin of his call removed the possibility of human error or the need for human approval.

Secondly, Paul writes, after a period of prayer, discernment and ministry, the community at Jerusalem and its leaders *did* endorse Paul's mission (2:1–21). The Council of Jerusalem, in about A.D. 50, authorized his ministry to the pagans without imposing the burden of the law. However sardonically, the apostolic assembly conceded that it "has been decided by the Holy Spirit and by ourselves not to saddle you [i.e., the pagan Christians] with any burden beyond [the] essentials" (Ac 15:28). This second point of Paul's apologia is that even though the Jerusalem authorities' approval of the Holy Spirit's revelation was not really necessary, it was given and, therefore, the inability of some members who were among the leaders (e.g., Cephas) to accept the implications of this revelation is indefensible. Just as the Jewish-Christian authorities were brought by grace to see the gospel's truth, so individual members must be brought into line with the decision approved by these authorities. This is the spirit in which Paul takes Cephas on before applying this lesson of history to the "mad" Galatians (Ga 3:1).

Galatians 1:6–10
A SUDDEN AND SEVERE WARNING

⁶ I am astonished at the promptness with which you have turned away from the one who called you and have decided to follow a differ- ⁷ ent version of the Good News. ·Not that there can be more than one Good News; it is merely that some troublemakers among you want to ⁸ change the Good News of Christ; ·and let me warn you that if anyone preaches a version of the Good News different from the one we have already preached to you, whether it be ourselves or an angel from heaven, he is to be ⁹ condemned. ·I am only repeating what we told you before: if anyone preaches a version of the Good News different from the one you have ¹⁰ already heard, he is to be condemned. ·So now whom am I trying to please—man, or God? Would you say it is men's approval I am looking for? If I still wanted that, I should not be what I am—a servant of Christ.

✠

In accusing tones, Paul reminds the Galatians that any change or shift of emphasis from the gospel he has preached is a turning away from the one God who has called them (1:6). By attempting to supplement the gospel with ordinances from the law (especially circumcision), the Galatians and their agitators are guilty of rejecting God. There is one, only one, version of the Good News (1:7–9; cf. 2 Co 11:4–6). Competition, compromise, comparisons, supplements are all just so many forms of idolatry. The most seductive of all temptations is to make grace less than grace by trying to make it more complicated, by using the addition and multiplication method. God's truth is simple. Outside agitators seem to have wanted the Galatians to add onto the gospel the works of the law. Paul's reaction might seem to be exaggerated when he says that by falling into this trap, the Galatians are rejecting God. This seems to be an overstatement. Is it not less risky for the agitators to say "More" when perhaps Paul has not said enough by saying "Less"? The agitators are not really subtracting by adding to the gospel. In the uncertain times of the first-century upheaval, the Galatians' agitators can perhaps be accused of being tutiorists (i.e., trying to be safe), but not idolators!

Perhaps uneasy because of the relative brevity of Paul's visit to them, the Galatians were especially susceptible to the agitators' suggestions that *had* he stayed with them longer, Paul would have surely shown them that the law and the gospel supplement each other. In his haste to evangelize them and then to press on to other communities, the agitators might have continued, Paul abridged the gospel and so cheated the Galatians. Perhaps, they contended, he presumed that others would provide the necessary supplement to his hurried teaching or, worse and still more threatening, might have counted the Galatian mission relatively insignificant and therefore not allotted it sufficient time and energy. So the agitators may have presented themselves to the Galatians as a kind of lifeline, a hopeful corrective to a too-simplistic version of the gospel. Thus, with such insinuations, the agitators undermined Paul's authority and the gospel in Galatia.

Paul answers these implicit accusations with insistence on the divine authority of his own vocation. He sets in opposition the possibility of serving God and pleasing people (1:10). Apparently, Paul would have been in terrible trouble in a popularity contest. His rating in the polls of public opinion would have devastated a more fragile self-image. Paul's audacity, nevertheless, does not stem from delusions of grandeur of an unrealistic self-concept. The gospel of God not only empowered but *compelled* Paul to preach (1 Co 9:16). Paul's confidence in this gospel does not come from his own brilliance or natural ability to grasp intellectual truths. Mindful of his own limitations, Paul says that if he himself changed, condensed or qualified the gospel, he would not just be in error, he would be condemned (Ga 1:8).

STUDY QUESTIONS: Discuss what you think Paul means by "a different version of the Good News." Do you think we live today amid different versions? If so, what are the differences and how is it they have appeal? Do you agree with Paul that there can be only one version? What is his version?

Galatians 1:11–24
PAUL'S CALL IS MISSION

¹¹ The fact is, brothers, and I want you to realize this, the Good News I preached is not a ¹² human message ·that I was given by men, it is something I learned only through a revela- ¹³ tion of Jesus Christ. ·You must have heard of my career as a practicing Jew, how merciless I was in persecuting the Church of God, how ¹⁴ how much damage I did to it, ·how I stood out among other Jews of my generation, and how enthusiastic I was for the traditions of my ancestors.

¹⁵ Then God, who had specially chosen me while I was still in my mother's womb, called ¹⁶ me through his grace and chose ·to reveal his Son in me, so that I might preach the Good News about him to the pagans. I did not stop ¹⁷ to discuss this with any human being, ·nor did I go up to Jerusalem to see those who were already apostles before me, but I went off to Arabia at once and later went straight back ¹⁸ from there to Damascus. ·Even when after three years I went up to Jerusalem to visit Cephas and stayed with him for fifteen days, ¹⁹ I did not see any of the other apostles; I only ²⁰ saw James, the brother of the Lord, ·and I swear before God that what I have just written ²¹ is the literal truth. ·After that I went to Syria ²² and Cilicia, ·and was still not known by sight ²³ to the churches of Christ in Judaea, ·who had heard nothing except that their onetime persecutor was now preaching the faith he had

24 previously tried to destroy; ·and they gave glory to God for me.

✠

Paul testifies that there is nothing of the gospel which is of his own making. As if to drive home this point, giving it its most cogent illustration, he recalls his past that earned him the reputation of bitter persecutor of the church (1:13–14, 23; Ph 3:6). So great was his zeal for the law of Moses, Paul reminds the Galatians, that it expressed itself in an ardent pursuit of those who were following the gospel way. His zeal could not contain itself but spilled over in tireless persecution of those whose faith presented a challenge, even a threat, to Judaism.

It is difficult to understand just why Paul's zeal for the law would have led him to persecute the Christians even before the tension between Jews and Christians became really acute. Judaism and Christianity, before the destruction of the Temple in A.D. 70, coexisted as minorities who recognized their common enemy as Rome. As long as they worshiped together in the Temple, there was some mutuality and identification between them. Antagonism between Judaism, which was based more and more exclusively on the law, and Christianity, which turned progressively to the pagan mission and went beyond the law, grew when the Temple no longer existed as a common meeting ground. But Paul testifies that he persecuted the church in the early years just after the death of Jesus and we need to try to understand why this was so.

The first century provided a climate of such unrest that Judaism acutely longed for a Messiah-leader who would rescue the Jews from the oppression of Rome. Many Jewish leaders emerged who promoted various ideas about how to assert and maintain national and religious independence. Some of these leaders were identified as the Messiah by the followers. And that was all right, for Judaism could absorb varying convictions about the meaning and the form that the salvation of the world would take. Followers of Jesus, therefore, were not unique in identifying a Messiah. Solely on this basis, Paul would probably not have felt compelled to hunt down and persecute any Jews simply because they had become followers of Jesus. But Jesus was no ordinary Messiah among others. Christians believed that Jesus, who submitted to the law by being put to death, challenged the law and revealed another way of salvation through the Resurrection. Before his conversion, Paul's problem with Christianity was that its claims for Jesus implied that the law was obsolete. After Paul's conversion, this was the very basis of Paul's own preaching (Rm 10:4). Formerly Paul's zeal for the law made him a persecutor of Christianity. Now his zeal for the gospel of Jesus helped him to see that the time of the law was over and the time of universal salvation, signified by the conversion of the pagans without the law, had come. But if Jesus had merely died, Christians might have ranked with the other disillusioned followers of sincere but impotent leaders. However, Jesus was, as

Paul puts it, "raised by God from the dead" (e.g., Ga 1:2; Rm 4:24–25, 6:4,9, 7:4, 8:11,34, 10:9). This supports the Christian claim that in Jesus God went beyond the law, annulling the verdict of the law by which Jesus was condemned to death. The law had cursed Jesus, putting him to death; and by submitting to this curse, Jesus brought the blessing of Abraham to the pagans (Ga 3:13–14). From Paul's testimony, we can make two observations about Paul's persecution of the church before his own conversion (around A.D. 35).

First, Paul apparently knew at least the rudiments of Christian teaching that would have prompted him to strive to quash Christianity as a potential threat to Judaism. Paul knew enough about the new religion to realize that it challenged the law he held so sacred. The law was already threatened by Roman oppression. Moreover, Judaism settled its own internal conflicts in terms of how the law was to be interpreted, while the Christians, Paul knew, followed a way of righteousness which, they claimed, went beyond that of the scribes and Pharisees (Mt 5:20). So Paul knew enough about Christianity to realize how potentially damaging this new belief was; but Paul did not know Jesus himself and he did not yet understand Christianity as gospel. Paul's experience illustrates a fundamentally significant difference between catechetics (i.e., teaching) and the power that the gospel is. Paul defines gospel as the power to save (Rm 1:16–17). In other words, to know facts about Jesus is not the same as knowing Jesus or, as Paul puts it, being "captured" by Jesus (Ph 3:12). Thus, Paul shows by the example of his own life that it is possible to know many facts before one is converted. Indeed, the facts not only did nothing to convert Paul, they amounted to sufficient cause for his active resistance and persecution of the fledgling church.

Secondly, Paul's zeal for the law could have prompted him to pursue the Christians because the law placed such strong emphasis on social, collective responsibility for its observance. That is, the law enjoined not only personal fidelity and conformity, but also such a deep sense of community that *all* were affected by its observance or by sins against it. The Old Testament is filled with examples of the collective effect of sin and of righteousness (as just one example, see the destruction of Sodom and Gomorrah in Gn 18:16–19:29). As a Jew, Paul realized that his obligation for the law's observance pertained not only to his own life but extended to responsibility for others. The Pharisees expressed their duty to protect the law with such technical phrases as "to build a fence around the law." Christians, however, were meanwhile preaching a Messiah whom the law condemned. The law, then, was threatened in the wake of this preaching. When Paul was called, he was also commissioned to preach to the pagans (Ga 2:7). His conversion to Jesus was at the same time conversion to the pagan mission. His sense of justice for the pagan was nourished by the Jewish sense of social responsibility. This would be incorporated into Paul's preaching mission. Just one practical example is Paul's emphasis on the contribution of money (Rm 15:22–33; 2 Co 8:1–9:15), which symbolized for him the pagans' full inclusion into the community as expressed by their substantial aid to the poor in Jerusalem. Conversion to Jesus implied, for Paul, responsibility to and for the church.

STUDY QUESTIONS: In describing his own call, Paul restates his conviction that it came through a revelation of Jesus Christ. Do you think there are any other ways that a person can be called to preach and teach the Good News? If so, what are they? How can a person *know* he or she has been called? Paul's story involves a dramatic change. Do you think people easily believed that Paul was a changed person? What kind of problems do you think Paul faced in his work?

Galatians 2:1-10
CREATING UNITY:
THE POOR AS THE CHURCH'S PRIORITY

¹ 2 It was not till fourteen years had passed that I went up to Jerusalem again. I went ² with Barnabas and took Titus with me. ·I went there as the result of a revelation, and privately I laid before the leading men the Good News as I proclaim it among the pagans; I did so for fear the course I was adopting or had already ³ adopted would not be allowed. ·And what happened? Even though Titus who had come with me is a Greek, he was not obliged to be cir- ⁴ cumcised. ·The question came up only because some who do not really belong to the brotherhood have furtively crept in to spy on the liberty we enjoy in Christ Jesus, and want to ⁵ reduce us all to slavery. ·I was so determined to safeguard for you the true meaning of the Good News, that I refused even out of deference to yield to such people for one moment. ⁶ As a result, these people who are acknowledged leaders—not that their importance matters to me, since God has no favorites—these leaders, as I say, had nothing to add to the ⁷ Good News as I preach it. ·On the contrary, they recognized that I had been commissioned to preach the Good News to the uncircumcised just as Peter had been commissioned to ⁸ preach it to the circumcised. ·The same person whose action had made Peter the apostle of the circumcised had given me a similar mission ⁹ to the pagans. ·So, James, Cephas and John,

these leaders, these pillars, shook hands with
Barnabas and me as a sign of partnership: we
were to go to the pagans and they to the cir-
¹⁰ cumcised. ·The only thing they insisted on was
that we should remember to help the poor, as
indeed I was anxious to do.

☩

Inspired by a second revelation (cf. 1:12 and 2:2)
following his initial conversion experience, Paul
went to Jerusalem fourteen years after he had first
visited Cephas there (1:17–2:1). In Jerusalem, the
gospel as Paul preached it to the pagans was
confirmed by the "pillars" of the church (i.e.,
James, Cephas and John, 2:9). The fact that Paul
briefly alternates in this passage between the use of
the Greek "Peter" and the Aramaic "Cephas" to
designate the same person can be confusing and
some explanation is necessary.

"Peter" is the Greek and "Cephas" the Aramaic
for "rock." According to the synoptic gospels, Jesus
changed Simon's name to Peter (Mt 16:18; Mk
3:16; Lk 6:14). John uses the Aramaic "Cephas" in
recording Jesus' change of Simon's name (Jn 1:42).
The name "Peter" appears in Paul's writings only in
Ga 2:7–8; elsewhere Paul refers to Cephas (1:18,
2:9,11,14; 1 Co 1:12, 9:5, 15:5). The most plausible explanation of this unique use of "Peter" in Ga
2:7–8 is that there Paul could be paraphrasing an
official decree issued by the Jerusalem authorities
which referred to Peter's mission to the circumcised
and Paul's to the uncircumcised. This decree, proba-

bly endorsed and promulgated by the Council of Jerusalem (Ac 15:1–35) and written in Greek, would have used the designation "Peter" which reflected the most general usage. Further, "Peter," as the name used by the authorities and known to the Galatians, would connote leadership; and Paul's point in Ga 2:7–8 is that his commission to preach to the pagans has equal status with the mission of Peter. Thus, when Paul is underscoring the equal authority of the Jewish and the pagan mission, he employs officially recognized nomenclature. But Paul himself retains preference for "Cephas" to which he returns in 2:9, in reference to the individual leader (rather than his mission). He repeats this less authoritative reference when he takes exception to Cephas' vacillating behavior in the wake of visits from "certain friends of James" (2:13).

The definitive decision made in Jerusalem was that there should be no further mistake about the validity of the pagan mission (2:7–9). The pagan converts were not to have second-class status in Christianity. Paul insists on the divine origin of his mission and authority. He does not need the other Christian leaders in order to give his own ministry legitimacy. His eagerness to have his mission confirmed by the Jewish-Christian leaders does not stem from personal insecurity or fear that his message is incomplete. His strong stance against Cephas and his bitter anger against those who are disturbing the Galatians is rooted in the belief that their position offends the gospel itself (2:5). Paul speaks with the passion of a missionary, more concerned that his readers be converted to the truth of the *gospel* than that they merely agree with *him*. Nourished by the vision of the prophetic tradition, Paul relies on the authority of his divine call and mission. He makes no excuses nor does he beg leave of any human authority.

As part of the doctrinal basis that underlies Paul's later description of the role of the law (3:1–4:31), Paul clarifies his authority first by reviewing his own call (1:11–24) and now by insisting on his position in the church (2:1–10). There is no inconsistency here—Paul does not *need* the authorities' approval for his mission, but the other Christian leaders need to recognize that Paul's mission is authorized by God. Paul is so emboldened by the revelation he received directly from God that, as he already showed, it is its own credential and it requires no further authorization (1:6–24). Yet Paul knows, too, that one of the essential duties of the Apostle is to keep the local community in touch with the Jerusalem authorities, and vice versa. The dynamism of Paul's task helps him to keep correcting and adjusting the vision of communities like those in Galatia as well as the integrity of those in Jerusalem. It is not enough for Paul to follow his own conscience or to respond to his own mission. In this regard, the significance of the Council of Jerusalem as well as the collection for the starving "saints" in Jerusalem is inestimable (1 Co 16:1–4; Rm 15:26–28). But the Council and the collection represent much more than simply open communication between the authorities and the missions. They also represent the vision that there is only one gospel and that all are included. If this is disputed or qualified at all, the gospel is threatened. And the gospel must correct Cephas (2:11–14) or James or the Galatian disturbers or Paul himself or even an angel (1:8)! The gospel needs no defense or authorization, but the community, local or universal, the leaders and individual Christians constantly must judge themselves by the measure of the gospel demand for universal salvation.

In the light of this absolutely essential and critical insight, Paul defends the pagan mission. For him this mission is a compelling expression of how the outcome of the Jerusalem Council can be summed up in the single mandate of giving priority to the needs of the poor (2:10). Paul's summary of this Council goes to the heart of the purpose for the minimal requirements that Ac 15:28–29 record. The pagans are not to be saddled with all kinds of restrictions that set them apart and limit charity as one among many obligations. As the former outcasts of Judaism, the pagans represent the poor to whom the gospel is now preached (cf. Lk 4:18, 7:22). The spiritually impoverished pagans draw closer to the financially impoverished saints in Jerusalem through the gospel. The Jerusalem Council, with its embrace of the pagan Christians, and the collection, which expressed the former pagans' care for the saints in Jerusalem, represent the mutual love the gospel demands. Recognition of the full incorporation of the pagans into Christianity is signified in even the Jewish-Christian authorities' amazing freedom to minimize the requirements of the law, subordinating them to the remembering to help the poor (Ga 2:10). Christian charity, empowered by the gospel, enables the Jerusalem community to treat the foreign poor (i.e., pagans) in the same gracious way the poor of Jerusalem are treated. That gospel insight is what makes the pagan mission symbolic. Actually, it seems, at least some of the pagans were in better financial shape than the "saints in Jerusalem." But the pagans represent the poor in that they are the acknowledged concern of both Paul and the Jerusalem authorities. The pagans thus signify the elimination of any distinction or exception to the gospel vision of universal salvation. The pagans, like the Jews, have access to grace through faith. Paul will oppose any attempt to lessen the impact of this gospel power. Thus his confrontation with Cephas, like his defense of his own authority, must not lead to division or jealousy. It is far more important than a conflict of personalities, a power struggle or a mere question of personal sensitivity. If the pagan mission, as symbol of charity and expression of the priority of the poor, is threatened, the gospel is threatened and the church's integrity is threatened.

Ga 2:1–10 lifts a veil so that we catch more than a glimpse of the behind-the-scenes tensions in the early church. There is a way of reading the history of the early church as Luke records it in Acts that allows us to miss the powerful differences within the community. An ideal picture seems to emerge from Acts if we draw an impression from the strategically placed summaries, such as the one in Ac 4:32–33:

> The whole group of believers was united, heart and soul; no one claimed for his own use anything that he had, as everything they owned was held in common.
> The apostles continued to testify to the resurrection

of the Lord Jesus with great power, and they were all given great respect.

But it would probably be a misunderstanding of Luke to exaggerate such summaries without considering the fact that in a following passage, to continue with this one example, he records the fraud of Ananias and Sapphira (5:1-11) and their terrible punishment because they withheld from the common property the proceeds of a sale. This deceit put them outside of the community. They died because they did not live the gospel's implications.

The reality of the early Christian community is that it experienced tensions and problems not so very different from problems of the church today: crises of leadership, with very real divisions among the authorities; crises of interpretation of law and morality and liturgy; tensions that were not superficial but that threatened the very fabric of community. Enter Paul with his sandpaper personality, an ardent pastor whose defense of the gospel, of himself and of his pagans seems to border on the fanatic! As he moves into high gear in describing the integrity of his gospel, his words about the established church leaders may be interpreted as sarcasm. But he is interested in the approval of pillars like Cephas, James and John because it attests to the truth of the gospel and helps to spread the true gospel (Ga 2:2). Only secondarily does Paul care that it also serves to silence his detractors and quiet the impressionable, besieged Galatians. Paul's appeal to the integrity of the authorities is part of his apostolic duty to make the truth also official.

STUDY QUESTIONS: What did Paul mean by saying "God has no favorites" (2:6)? How have we identified ourselves as Christians? Using what symbols? Is this good? Why? What is the role of authority in the church? How does the church minister to the poor today? Do you concur with Paul that we will be watering down the gospel if the poor are not our first priority?

Galatians 2:11–14
THE TRUTH IN CONFRONTATION

¹¹ When Cephas came to Antioch, however, I opposed him to his face, since he was mani-
¹² festly in the wrong. ·His custom had been to eat with the pagans, but after certain friends of James arrived he stopped doing this and kept away from them altogether for fear of
¹³ the group that insisted on circumcision. ·The other Jews joined him in this pretense, and even Barnabas felt himself obliged to copy their behavior.
¹⁴ When I saw they were not respecting the true meaning of the Good News, I said to Cephas in front of everyone, "In spite of being a Jew, you live like the pagans and not like the Jews, so you have no right to make the pagans copy Jewish ways."

☩

Tradition holds that Cephas, as Paul prefers to call Peter, was the founder and an indisputable authority of the church at Antioch. Antioch had probably the largest Jewish settlement outside of Israel at the time; therefore the prominent church of Antioch was undoubtedly Jewish-Christian in the main. It was in Antioch that followers of Jesus were first called "Christians" (Ac 11:19–26).

Here, in Cephas' own sphere of authority, Paul

boldly confronted him, accusing him of living a lie because of fear (Ga 2:11–12). According to Paul, Cephas jeopardized the gospel's freedom from the law. It would require no great effort of the imagination to understand why this might have happened: peer pressure, a natural reluctance on Cephas' part to risk his own reputation or shirk his own leadership role or even such a commendable motive as not wishing to proceed so quickly that some might be scandalized. Add any or all of these to Cephas' probable anxiety to show deference to James who was the leader of the church in Jerusalem and we have ample reason to understand why Cephas wanted to be cautious and to reconsider his own and the others' preliminary, enthusiastic impulse for total freedom of the gospel from the law.

According to Paul's own witness in this passage, it is not as if Cephas denied some established tenets of the gospel's preaching. Cephas' offense is overprudence, which amounts, in Paul's view, to falsifying the gospel and leading others astray. The gospel means freedom from the barriers religion naturally erects between people. Paul emphasizes that fellowship at the meal table, while contrary to Jewish law, represents the gospel's repudiation of all boundaries: all in Christ are one (3:28).

STUDY QUESTIONS: Is it only because Cephas seems to be inconsistent that Paul accuses him of being "wrong"? Is it appropriate for a person to say someone else (especially one in an authority or leadership role) is wrong? Paul claims to know the "true meaning" of the Good News. Do you agree that he did? What do you think is that "true meaning"?

Galatians 2:15–21
THE FAITH THAT SAVES

15 Though we were born Jews and not pagan
16 sinners, ·we acknowledge that what makes a man righteous is not obedience to the Law, but faith in Jesus Christ. We had to become believers in Christ Jesus no less than you had, and now we hold that faith in Christ rather than fidelity to the Law is what justifies us, and that no one can be justified by keeping the
17 Law. ·Now if we were to admit that the result of looking to Christ to justify us is to make us sinners like the rest, it would follow that Christ had induced us to sin, which would be absurd.
18 If I were to return to a position I had already abandoned, I should be admitting I had done
19 something wrong. ·In other words, through the Law I am dead to the Law, so that now I can live for God. I have been crucified with Christ,
20 and I live now not with my own life but with the life of Christ who lives in me. The life I now live in this body I live in faith: faith in the Son of God who loved me and who sacri-
21 ficed himself for my sake. ·I cannot bring myself to give up God's gift: if the Law can justify us, there is no point in the death of Christ.

✠

Paul maintains that what the Jews and pagan sinners have in common is that they both come to the same conviction of faith in Christ (2:15-16). Jews and pagans both strive for righteousness, but now, through Christ, they realize that this cannot be achieved through the law. Although the Jews tried the way of the law, it did not justify them. They, no less than the pagans, conclude that righteousness is achieved through faith. This righteousness is more than a revelation of their sinful condition, for, as Paul implies, if knowledge of our sinfulness is the only result of faith, then faith is absurd, extraneous, unnecessary (2:17). The law had already revealed the universality of sin (Ps 14:1-3; Rm 3:9). "Through the Law, I am dead to the Law," Paul says, so that now "I live in faith" (Ga 2:19-20). Thus faith goes beyond the law, for if by faith we do no more than return to the conclusion of the law, this would imply that faith is wrong (3:18). The law convicts us of sin and kills us; by faith we live for God. Paul views two mutually exclusive spheres of human existence, the law and faith (2:19). If the law prevails or if the law were sufficient, there would be no need for Christ's death (3:21).

Through Christ, we have died to our former way of life, regardless of the values it may have represented. Like his contemporaries Paul divided humankind into two groups: Jews and pagans, the latter term a synonym for "sinners." In passages of other epistles (e.g., Rm 3:9-20), Paul stresses the sinfulness of both groups; that is, he emphasizes that *all* have sinned. In our passage in Galatians, Paul's point is a complementary one. The Jews have access to grace only through faith in Christ, no less than the Gentiles do. At times Paul alludes to the former privilege of the Jews because of the law (Rm 3:1-8,

9:1-5; Ph 3:5-6). Here in Galatians, partly in reaction to the agitators who threatened the Galatian communities and partly because he had come to understand the relationship between faith and the law as antithetical, Paul insists that possessing the law does not in any way lessen the demand for faith. As Paul explains in Ph 3:7, the advantage of the law is now for him disadvantage. The law, which previously Paul himself counted advantage, created blindness on the part of the Jews to their need for grace (cf. Rm 10:2-3). Paradoxically, the disadvantage of the pagans' sinfulness, on the other hand, made them more receptive to faith, thereby giving them the advantage.

Paul's real insight, however, goes beyond whatever may formerly have been considered either advantage or disadvantage before God as a basis of division among people. In Christ, as Paul says so eloquently in 2 Co 5:17, "the old creation has gone, and now the new one is here." We are a "new creature" (Ga 6:15); we become a community, a people, the "Israel of God" (6:16). Quite simply put, "in Christ" all human barriers (e.g., birthright, privilege, law, etc.) are nullified (cf. 3:28). Even "born Jews" such as Paul, Cephas or James must acknowledge that obedience to the law counts for nothing. Now all are judged in the light of the new life of faith. Apparently, Ga 2:19-21 originally came out of a baptismal context. Through Baptism, Christians are dead to the law. The life of faith they now live devalues all that preceded faith. This new life reveals the truth of the gospel.

Not only Baptism, but even the Old Testament

says that sin is universal (Ps 14:1-3, 143:2; Rm 3:10-20). Under the law itself, the Jews as well as pagans are identified as sinners. The law itself also provides for the fact that it cannot be fully obeyed by all the people all the time. For example, the required sin offerings (Lv 4:1-7:38) and the general observance of the Day of Atonement (Lv 16:1-34) testify to the impossibility of achieving righteousness by the simple possession of the law. Although the law must be kept, its possession does not include the power for Israel to observe it. Thus, it is not only faith in Christ that reveals human sinfulness; the law does, too. And faith goes beyond the law, beyond the need to convict us of sin. Righteousness comes from faith.

Human reasoning might argue that faith in Christ seems to imply that Christ is an agent of sin (Ga 2:17). Hence, knowledge of Christ, if this reasoning is followed, seems to multiply our sinfulness. But this is absurd. It represents a kind of reasoning that is completely opposed to the Christians' converted state of mind. Paul holds that there are two kinds of fools—those who understand the logical philosophies of this world but are blind to the realities of the world to come and those who are fools for the sake of Christ (1 Co 4:10) but unknowledgeable in the ways of this world. It is not that faith is opposed to knowledge but that faith is a different *kind* of knowledge. Clearly, Paul's thinking is connected to human experience and reasoning, but it is most fundamentally *determined* by the revelation of God, a wisdom that is *given* and not the result of human effort or study. God's wisdom not only renders any possibility of a return to an unconverted state incomprehensible, but also makes such a return impossible. Through the law, we (Paul uses the collective "I" of experience in Romans 7) have already died to the law and to sin. If dead, we cannot live under sin any longer.

STUDY QUESTIONS: Is "faith in Christ" enough? How does a person act out faith in Jesus Christ? Is there any relationship between the law and faith in Jesus Christ? Do we need any religious rules or church law? Why? How do we apply faith to observance of the law?

Galatians 3:1–9
THE GIFT OF THE SPIRIT

¹ 3 Are you people in Galatia mad? Has someone put a spell on you, in spite of the plain explanation you have had of the crucifixion of ² Jesus Christ? ·Let me ask you one question: was it because you practiced the Law that you received the Spirit, or because you believed ³ what was preached to you? ·Are you foolish enough to end in outward observances what ⁴ you began in the Spirit? ·Have all the favors you received been wasted? And if this were so, they would most certainly have been wasted. ⁵ Does God give you the Spirit so freely and work miracles among you because you practice the Law, or because you believed what was preached to you?

⁶ Take Abraham for example: he put his faith in God, and this faith was considered as justi- ⁷ fying him. ·Don't you see that it is those who rely on faith who are the sons of Abraham? ⁸ Scripture foresaw that God was going to use faith to justify the pagans, and proclaimed the Good News long ago when Abraham was told: ⁹ In you all the pagans will be blessed. ·Those therefore who rely on faith receive the same blessing as Abraham, the man of faith.

✠

Paul continues to develop the theme of discernment, asking if the Galatians are mad (3:1; cf. 3:3), challenging them to a self-examination on the absurdity of their position. Do they act with faith or from fear? Do they wish to conform to the law that their own experience has taught them is obsolete? They are being tempted to try to complement faith in Christ with works of the law. This is equivalent to saying that they must complete the gift of the Spirit, as if God's gift is somehow insufficient. Or, as Paul challenged in 2:21, do they suppose that Christ's death were to no avail? The critical point that distinguishes wisdom from madness is not logical deduction but consistency with grace. To depart from God's free grace is folly.

The Galatians, Paul insists, received the Spirit through faith-filled hearing. They were sufficiently free to submit, to obey, to receive and experience "miracles" (3:5) of the gospel. It would be madness, then, to think of returning to the slavery of works of the law or to assume that what God began through miracles and gift needs to be completed by regression to legal requirements (3:3). Paul cannot be more forceful than when he resorts to the antithesis of faith and law by which he defines the sanity of God's wisdom and opposes the best human systems as madness (3:5).

It is the epitome of madness to have seen clearly the lesson of Christ's death and to forget it by averting one's eyes from the cross. On this point the Greek is more powerfully picturesque than our translation. In Greek, the image of the crucified Jesus was painted before the very eyes of the Galatians (cf. 3:1). Jesus' death was not merely explained to them; they witnessed its truth, awful and unforgettable. The stark realism of the gospel's message is that, condemned by people of the law, Jesus was delivered into the hands of sinful people (e.g., Mt 26:59–68, 27:1–2; Ac 2:22–23, 3:13–26). The Jews and pagans together (i.e., all people) share responsibility for Jesus' death, a death that saved them all. The fact that Jesus' death is redemptive is the insight of faith. Paul states faith's teaching simply: "Christ died for our sins" (1 Co 15:3). Once received, faith cannot be reversed. Though the Galatians may not have witnessed Jesus' death in Jerusalem, the truth of the crucifixion was virtually fixed before their eyes by the preaching of the gospel. That is the thrust of Paul's conviction that the gospel is the *power* of salvation rather than a merely human invention or recitation of history or clever propaganda (cf. Rm 1:16–17).

As in Romans 4, Paul portrays Abraham in Galatians 3 as the man of faith (3:6–9). The inheritance he left is faith. His influence goes beyond a race or a certain group of people. Abraham for Paul is the most positive figure of the Old Testament. Preceding the law, Abraham shows the meaning of justification by faith without the law. By being unaware of the law, Abraham avoids its contamination. Thus he demonstrates by clear example that faith without the law justifies.

STUDY QUESTIONS: Paul makes faith sound very simple. Do you agree that faith is indeed that simple? What is the role of the Spirit according to Paul? How do we test the Spirit?

Galatians 3:10–14
LAW, THE ANTITHESIS OF FAITH

10 On the other hand, those who rely on the keeping of the Law are under a curse, since scripture says: Cursed be everyone who does not persevere in observing everything pre-
11 scribed in the book of the Law. ·The Law will not justify anyone in the sight of God, because we are told: the righteous man finds life
12 through faith. ·The Law is not even based on faith, since we are told: The man who practices these precepts finds life through practic-
13 ing them. ·Christ redeemed us from the curse of the Law by being cursed for our sake, since scripture says: Cursed be everyone who is
14 hanged on a tree. ·This was done so that in Christ Jesus the blessing of Abraham might include the pagans, and so that through faith we might receive the promised Spirit.

✠

Paul's thesis in this doctrinal part of Galatians (3:1–4:31) is that justification comes through faith alone, not through the law (see also Rm 4:1–25). The Old Testament person studied the law to learn how to become just. Justification, in other words, is one's goal in following the way of the law. But the law, Paul argues, could not justify anyone in the sight of God. Justification is, for Paul, a concept based on a forensic image, a courtroom, so to speak, in which the accused expect the verdict "Guilty." There is evidence of universal sin; all, Jews and pagans alike, expect to be condemned. The law itself is admitted to testify to this verdict. But the judgment of God is that all are justified through faith. This is the surprise of grace that overthrows the law's condemnation. Thus, faith and the verdict of the law are opposites. As clearly as the law necessarily condemns, faith leads to justification (see the discussion of Rm 1:16–17, p. 134).

In Ga 3:10–14 Paul draws further implications for his law-faith antithesis proposed in 3:1–5. Not only can the law not justify, it places all who submit to it under a curse. The Apostle shares with his contemporaries a world view that sees humans as guided by some spiritual force. One is dominated either by the spirit of good (for Paul, faith or grace) or the spirit of evil (the law, sin). Humans must serve one of these, good or evil. Our free choice is limited by what spirit we serve. If we are under the law, we are subject to all its dictates. Human actions, according to Jewish liturgy and belief, bring either blessings or curses. The law says on the one hand that all who fail to observe its commands are cursed (Dt 27:26; Ga 3:10). Yet the Old Testament also testifies that *no one* is justified by observing all the law's commands (e.g., Ps 14:1–3). Even the one who strives most faithfully to keep the law, indeed even Christ himself, is under the curse of the law (Ga 3:10,13).

The term "curse" becomes a key word which links the hopeless situation of all those who rely on the law (3:10) to the hope of redemption in Christ (3:13). Jesus himself submits to the curse of the law, and by his death rendered the law (with its curse) void: "Now the Law has come to an end with Christ" (Rm 10:4). God, in Jesus, went beyond the jurisdiction of the law, which could not do more than sentence Jesus to death. But God raised Jesus from the dead and accomplished what the law was unable to do, that is, satisfy the just demands of the law and give us the promised spirit (8:3–4). In Christ, the promise given to Abraham was fulfilled and the way of salvation was opened to all who are descendants of Abraham through faith (Ga 3:14). Since the promise is greater than the law (3:15–29), it cannot be limited by the law which excludes the pagans. By faith, all (pagans included) receive the Spirit who was promised (3:14). Paul's reference here to the Spirit received through faith can remind us of the absurdity of trying to return to the way of the law rendered futile by the gift of faith and the Spirit freely bestowed (cf. 3:3,5).

STUDY QUESTIONS: How do the death and the Resurrection of Jesus reverse the verdict of the law's condemnation to death? How can Christian hope operate in a person's life and bring life to others?

Galatians 3:15–18
THE LAW DICTATES BUT
NEITHER PROMISES NOR EMPOWERS

¹⁵ Compare this, brothers, with what happens in ordinary life. If a will has been drawn up in due form, no one is allowed to disregard it
¹⁶ or add to it. ·Now the promises were addressed to Abraham and to his descendants—notice, in passing, that scripture does not use a plural word as if there were several descendants, it uses the singular: to his posterity, which is
¹⁷ Christ. ·But my point is this: once God had expressed his will in due form, no law that came four hundred and thirty years later could cancel that and make the promise meaningless.
¹⁸ If you inherit something as a legal right, it does not come to you as the result of a promise, and it was precisely in the form of a promise that God made his gift to Abraham.

☩

Paul uses the analogy of a legal will to show the priority of the promise made to Abraham over the law of Moses (3:15,17). In the Old Testament this promise was presented as a contract, a "will," a testament. It was a kind of agreement, although unequal in terms, because it bound two unequal parties, God and Israel. God was held to the agreement's terms just as the people were. The repeated witness of the prophets, often expressed in ominous terms, was that the consequences of the people's infidelity in view of God's fidelity, brought judgment on the people.

Paul's audience understood this example out of its own experience. A contract is binding even in death. When a person dies, an agreement expressed in a duly executed and authorized will has to be honored. Death provides the conditions that illustrate the will's binding power. Paul applies his analogy to the relationship between the promise and the law. The promise expresses the terms of God's will; the law was meant to make these terms more explicit. God's promise predated the law. God called Abraham and promised him a land. Blessing him, God promised to make Abraham a great nation (Gn 12:1–2). Only four hundred and thirty years later did the law appear (Ga 3:17). Paul's dating is probably based on Ex 12:40–41, although chronology is beside the point. Paul refers to a rabbinic rule of interpretation which dictates that whatever precedes according to scripture takes precedence in reality and therefore in value. The purpose of the law when it came was to expose the conditions of the promise. And even though the law was ineffective in achieving this purpose, it could not make the promise void. Paul gives two cogent reasons.

First, it would be absurd to suppose that a later intervention could nullify the original terms of the will (i.e., the promise). And secondly, the promise was given by God, the stronger party to the agreement. The conditions for the law's fulfillment were met in Christ who submitted to the law. But more. The conditions for the promise's fulfillment were met in Christ, the descendant of Abraham (Ga 3:16). And we inherit the fulfillment of the promise in Christ.

STUDY QUESTIONS: What promises of God were unaffected by the law? In what sense is promise outside of law?

Galatians 3:19–22
THE LIMITS OF THE LAW

¹⁹ What then was the purpose of adding the Law? This was done to specify crimes, until the posterity came to whom the promise was addressed. The Law was promulgated by angels, assisted by an intermediary. ·Now there ²⁰ can only be an intermediary between two parties, ²¹ yet God is one. ·Does this mean that there is opposition between the Law and the promises of God? Of course not. We could have been justified by the Law if the Law we were ²² given had been capable of giving life, ·but it is not: scripture makes no exceptions when it says that sin is master everywhere. In this way the promise can only be given through faith in Jesus Christ and can only be given to those who have this faith.

✠

The law revealed sin but could not enable anyone to conquer sin. Paul speaks similarly in Romans 7. There he develops at greater length his response to the question raised here in Ga 3:19: "What then is the purpose of adding the Law?" Although the law itself is holy, it demonstrated the power of sin. It showed us what is right but was not able to help us do what is right. Thus the law acted as an agent of sin and condemned us. The law in fact contributed ment. The conditions for the law's fulfillment were met in Christ who submitted to the law. But more. The conditions for the promise's fulfillment were met in Christ, the descendant of Abraham (Ga 3:16). And we inherit the fulfillment of the promise in Christ.

STUDY QUESTIONS: What promises of God were unaffected by the law? In what sense is promise outside of law?

Galatians 3:19-22
THE LIMITS OF THE LAW

¹⁹ What then was the purpose of adding the Law? This was done to specify crimes, until the posterity came to whom the promise was addressed. The Law was promulgated by an- ²⁰ gels, assisted by an intermediary. ·Now there can only be an intermediary between two par- ²¹ ties, yet God is one. ·Does this mean that there is opposition between the Law and the promises of God? Of course not. We could have been justified by the Law if the Law we were ²² given had been capable of giving life, ·but it is not: scripture makes no exceptions when it says that sin is master everywhere. In this way the promise can only be given through faith in Jesus Christ and can only be given to those who have this faith.

☩

The law revealed sin but could not enable anyone to conquer sin. Paul speaks similarly in Romans 7. There he develops at greater length his response to the question raised here in Ga 3:19: "What then is the purpose of adding the Law?" Although the law itself is holy, it demonstrated the power of sin. It showed us what is right but was not able to help us do what is right. Thus the law acted as an agent of sin and condemned us. The law in fact contributed to the helplessness of our plight when we were as yet without faith. Sin defines the limits of the law. Only faith can remove these limits.

The law was limited in two respects: time and the means of its promulgation (3:19). Paul's argument is based on rabbinic assumptions and his procedure is *a fortiori* (i.e., "if such and such is true, how much more true is . . ."). The promise, coming before the law, takes precedence over the law. The promise, furthermore, was given by God, whereas the law was promulgated by intermediaries (i.e., the literal meaning of "angels" in Greek). The notion of the mediation by angels seems to be rooted in the transcendence of God so that there appears to be an insistence on a distinction between God and his messengers, especially in some Old Testament traditions. This notion of the law's being mediated by angels, although not explicit in the Old Testament itself, is alluded to in some other New Testament texts (Ac 7:38,53; Heb 2:2). Paul uses the theme of the mediation of angels in Ga 3:19 to show the relative inferiority of the law compared to the promise which was directly given by God.

The idea behind Ga 3:20 seems to be highly complex and technical. Perhaps the best explanation, however, is a simple one. The law given by Moses clearly implies the necessity for an intermediary, a function either Moses or the law itself fulfills. An intermediary in turn implies a lack of directness. The law and Moses represent the necessity for a go-between who will facilitate some kind of dialogue between the two parties involved (i.e., between God and Israel). An intermediary can also complicate communication if there exists some misunderstanding about his role in bringing about agreement. The mediator can have too much prominence, for example, and be seen as an end in himself rather than as a means. So, the role of the law came to be misused. The law imposed conditions. But the promise supersedes the law because it is freely given by the stronger party to the agreement, that is, by God. And it is given without terms. Appealing to rabbinic reasoning and values, Paul argues that the promise of the "one" is better than an agreement between two parties which requires an intermediary. Thus the promise outvalues the law.

STUDY QUESTIONS: How does Paul describe the relationship between sin, the law, faith and the promise? Can you identify the rabbinic presuppositions Paul uses to show the law's limits and inferiority to the promise?

Galatians 3:23-29
FAITH'S COMING OF AGE

23 Before faith came, we were allowed no freedom by the Law; we were being looked after
24 till faith was revealed. ·The Law was to be our guardian until the Christ came and we could be
25 justified by faith. ·Now that that time has come
26 we are no longer under that guardian, ·and you are, all of you, sons of God through faith in
27 Christ Jesus. ·All baptized in Christ, you have
28 all clothed yourselves in Christ, ·and there are no more distinctions between Jew and Greek, slave and free, male and female, but all of you
29 are one in Christ Jesus. ·Merely by belonging to Christ you are the posterity of Abraham, the heirs he was promised.

☩

Abandoning for the moment his analogy of the will (3:15-18), Paul adapts the image of a guardian which he will briefly introduce here (3:23-26) and continue in 4:1-11. As a teacher, Paul realizes that an illustration from everyday life is invaluable. Paul uses the guardian image to help explain the role of the law. He reaches for analogies that will express the power of God's promise realized in Jesus in contrast to the relative impotence of the law. Paul thus betrays a certain ambivalence in himself about the law, an ambivalence that we can easily understand when we remember the zeal for the law that characterized his Jewish past. His conversion to Christ did not eliminate but redirected this zeal. His ambivalence has roots in his concern for his own people (see Romans 9–11) coupled with his call to go out and become the Apostle to the pagans. Temporarily, at least, he must abandon his own people to pursue his mission to the pagans. The argument about the role of the law, nevertheless, has particular impact for this Jewish Apostle to the pagans.

The guardian image Paul borrows from his Greco-Roman world. It was a custom in that world for the wealthy to assign a slave as guardian to the sons of the household. The duties of the guardian were numerous, ranging from tutoring to insuring the physical safety of the boy who would one day be the heir and master. Although socially inferior, then, to their charges, these guardians temporarily exercised authority over their future masters until they reached the age of maturity as determined by the boy's father. By analogy, Paul understands the role of the law (Ga 3:24). Like the guardian, the law dictated our actions, watched over us and exercised authority over us until the time was ripe for the revelation of faith in and through Christ. As guardian, the law's custody was temporary. But now, since Christ has come, the role of the law is no longer relevant. Formerly we were allowed no freedom (3:23). Now we are declared heirs, children of God through faith (3:25–26,29). Now is the time for the heirs to receive the inheritance promised to them all along. The guardian could do nothing to prevent the inheritance; his role was only to insure that the time of the inheritance would come. The law, having served this function, holds sway no longer.

An essential characteristic of this inheritance is freedom from all binding and destructive divisions. In 3:28 Paul testifies that in Christ all the inequalities constructed by an immature society still under the guardianship of the law are removed. He identifies the unequal parties vulnerable to discrimination in the society of his time—Jews and pagans (each group being considered inferior by the other), slaves and women. These socially recognized inequalities are eliminated by Baptism, which Paul is often alluding to when he uses the phrase "in Christ" (3:28; cf. Rm 6:3-5,11, 8:1, 12:5; 1 Co 6:11 and passim). Obviously, Paul is not referring merely to the rite of Baptism, but to the Christian reality of Baptism which he believes transforms lives. Through Baptism the otherwise normal human divisions become obsolete and irrelevant. The unity which exists among Christians must transcend the natural divisions of religion, social status, sex. The corresponding pairs Jew-Gentile, slave-free are associated in other New Testament texts (cf. 1 Co 12:13; Col 3:11). For Paul, the point is that with the coming of Christ and faith, a new creation is formed that affects all relationships and makes union possible, not only with Christ but also with one another.

With the coming of age through Baptism, Paul then implies, comes the passing of anything that may have handicapped the heir's full acceptance of the inheritance. Our world admits a multitude of handicaps: age, sex, religion, social or economic status, political affiliation. The gist of Paul's analogy is that all such divisions belong to the world of the minor's tutelage, when the heir was not yet able to receive the promise because the guardian's tenure had not yet expired. But, as Paul goes on to show, Christ brought the fullness of the promise and thus announced the time of the guardian-law's ineffectiveness regarding the heirs. *All* are heirs, equal in the terms of the promise, under Christ.

This passage is particularly apt for showing how concrete and practical is Paul's application of the priority of the command to "love your neighbor" which he presents as a summary of the law (Rm 13:9–10; Ga 5:14; cf. Lv 19:18). Love of neighbor provides the basis for Paul's absolute insistence on the gospel's inclusion of everyone, with no divisions possible. Whereas the ordinances of the law distinguished among the Jew and pagan, slave and free, male and female, the love command gathers and unifies. The vision of universal inheritance cannot be compromised. Thus Paul rejects, without qualification, any divisions on the grounds of race, sex, economic or social domination. He declares himself a prophet for all times in refusing to allow any exceptions to this radical gospel mandate. He challenges us to tear down, as "guardians" that enslave, any barriers that are erected. The peace we build can only be an expression of recognizing *all* as the inheritors of the promises of justice.

STUDY QUESTIONS: How is it possible that there was a time *before* faith? What does

Paul mean by being "clothed . . . in Christ" (Ga 3:27)? Is our faith mature? What are the barriers to our coming of age in the church? Does any racial, national or sexual prejudice still make us spiritually impotent? In the church? In the world? What keeps us from accepting that "others"—those not like ourselves—receive the full inheritance of faith? Give examples of divisions among people that challenge the church to apply Paul's vision of "universal inclusivism" (cf. Introduction, pp. 25–27).

Galatians 4:1–11
BORN OF GOD'S OWN LIFE

¹ **4** Let me put this another way: an heir, even if he has actually inherited everything, is no different from a slave for as long as he re- ² mains a child. ·He is under the control of guardians and administrators until he reaches ³ the age fixed by his father. ·Now before we came of age we were as good as slaves to the ⁴ elemental principles of this world, ·but when the appointed time came, God sent his Son, born of a woman, born a subject of the Law, ⁵ to redeem the subjects of the Law and to en- ⁶ able us to be adopted as sons. ·The proof that you are sons is that God has sent the Spirit of his Son into our hearts: the Spirit that cries, ⁷ "Abba, Father," ·and it is this that makes you a son, you are not a slave any more; and if God has made you son, then he has made you heir.

⁸ Once you were ignorant of God, and enslaved to "gods" who are not really gods at all; ⁹ but now that you have come to acknowledge God—or rather, now that God has acknowledged you—how can you want to go back to elemental things like these, that can do nothing ¹⁰ and give nothing, and be their slaves? ·You and your special days and months and seasons and ¹¹ years! ·You make me feel I have wasted my time with you.

☩

Paul has emphasized the implications of Christ's coming in the fullness of time (3:27-29). Here in 4:1-11 he returns to the guardian image of 3:23-26, drawing out the implications of the temporary role of the law and the comparative fullness of freedom of the children-heirs of the promise, a fullness that is all the more appreciated when it is contrasted with the previous limitations of the minor (4:1-2).

Paul underscores the idea that our coming of age is not dependent upon any other conditions of maturity than a paternal decision of God, the Father (4:4). A father determines the moment his children will become heirs (4:2). At that time, child is enabled to inherit by the power of the father's own free will for benevolence. Paul's "proof" is attested by our ability to recognize God as Father, an ability given by the Spirit of Jesus (4:6; see also Rm 8:14-17). Not merely through example but by the empowering effect of the reconciliation of the cross, Jesus taught us to call God "Abba," that is, "Daddy." This is no mere title or metaphor. It is a name that enables; it reveals the intimately personal depth of relationship and common life won through Jesus' sacrifice.

Reflecting the patriarchal heritage of his culture and religion, Paul naturally employed masculine language which, although it was not offensive to him, nevertheless presents some difficulty for us today. Having just insisted on the unity of all in Christ, it is not possible that Paul could have meant to indulge a sexist bias either in his reference to God as "Father" or in his designation of Christians as "sons" of God. If we are to understand Paul at all, we must be able to see that he consistently appeals to unity while rejecting division. This appeal transcends all apparent bias. The Apostle's intention is manifestly inclusive. The coming of age of the children of the promise marks the time of God's recognition of all, not just some, as heirs.

Once we have come of age, there can be no going back, no regressing to rely again on the law, on elemental spirits, on the powers of this world as opposed to the freedom of real children (Ga 4:3,8–9). In Romans, Paul used the image of death as a way of showing the impossibility of returning to a former state (e.g., Rm 6:2). Now he has shown the new identity that the former minors have acquired by becoming heirs. It is as impossible for them to return to their former state as it would be to reverse death.

STUDY QUESTIONS: Is the experience of the law that Paul describes as universal as he implies? In what form does the Spirit's identification of us as the children of God find expression? How do we experience "proof" that we are the children of God?

Galatians 4:12–20
PASSING ON THE LIFE OF GOD

¹² Brothers, all I ask is that you should copy me as I copied you. You have never treated ¹³ me in an unfriendly way before; ·even at the beginning, when that illness gave me the opportunity to preach the Good News to you, ¹⁴ you never showed the least sign of being revolted or disgusted by my disease that was such a trial to you; instead you welcomed me as an angel of God, as if I were Christ Jesus ¹⁵ himself. ·What has become of this enthusiasm you had? I swear that you would even have gone so far as to pluck out your eyes and give ¹⁶ them to me. ·Is it telling you the truth that has ¹⁷ made me your enemy? ·The blame lies in the way they have tried to win you over: by separating you from me, they want to win you over ¹⁸ to themselves. ·It is always a good thing to win people over—and I do not have to be there with ¹⁹ you—but it must be for a good purpose, ·my children! I must go through the pain of giving birth to you all over again, until Christ is ²⁰ formed in you. ·I wish I were with you now so that I could know exactly what to say; as it is, I have no idea what to do for the best.

✠

There is a way of superficially hearing Paul that can almost shock us when we consider his audacity.

Imagine ourselves having the nerve to suggest to others—our children, our students or other dependents or friends—that they imitate us (4:12; cf. 1 Co 11:1; Ph 4:9; 2 Th 3:7)! Even if we might be so bold as to suggest that they copy us in doing a certain thing the way we do or manifest certain behavior under certain circumstances, it seems a personally petrifying proposition to me that anyone should actually know and observe all that I do and follow exactly my example. Yet this is precisely what Paul enjoins the Galatians to do. This is the kind of openness, integrity and honesty Paul reflects in his own life and ministry and which he puts out as a challenge to anyone who would claim to be a minister in his tradition. In a very real sense, there is no way of superficially understanding Paul; the demands inherent in his words have to be pondered in order to be understood at all, much less practiced.

Paul never gets very far away from speaking personally, from putting his own life on the line. He has "objectively" appealed to the Galatians' experience. Now he reminds them of the experiences he himself has shared with them. They should recall how they themselves treated the Apostle when he was with them—in fact, when they first met him. There they have a point of reference and comparison for understanding God's own gratuitous love. Those who have ever tended someone who was ill or who have been ill and received love have experienced the mystery of undeserved love, a love that unites minister and sufferer.

It would probably be futile and at best irrelevant to try to discover the nature of Paul's illness or disease. He is said to have been afflicted with everything from alcoholism to extreme ugliness or a physical deformity of some kind. We can remember his own reference to a "thorn in the flesh"—some suffering he was given, he says, to keep him from becoming too proud (2 Co 12:7). Any sickness can seem to be particularly disgusting (Paul's implication in Ga 4:14) to those who suffer from it. We need only reflect on some of the most threatening modern-day ailments that victimize members of almost every family to identify closely with an experience that Paul designates as a fundamental part of his personal history with the Galatians. Healer that he is, Paul was introduced to this community as wounded, needing medical attention and long-term care, acceptance and patient friendliness. Even if Paul could point to his past history with the Thessalonians and the Corinthians as a productive, contributing resident in their midst (cf. Ac 18:1-3; 1 Co 9:11-12; 2 Th 3:7-9), such a luxury with its attending self-confidence and feeling of accomplishment is not the case in Galatia. When the Galatians met Paul, he was sick, dependent, without illusion or pretense—or possibility of these (Ga 4:13-15). And they received him, Paul reminds them, with exquisite sensitivity, with disarming simplicity and a total lack of defensiveness. Their former reception is a kind of challenging prod to their conscience to hear him now.

Drawing on probably the most compelling relationship images he could ever have found, Paul speaks of himself as a mother enduring the birth pangs twice for this erring community (3:19). A real mother might protest that she would willingly, and in fact, forget the pains of giving birth in view of the joy she has in beholding her child (Jn 16:21). Yet few might risk asking the question, right in the midst of her pain, whether it was all worthwhile. And the question becomes more sensitive and tenuous if the children become worrisome, as they begin to create problems, go through crises, become ungrateful adults. Yet, even given this kind of a choice, under these circumstances, as it were, Paul answers affirmatively. His "birth pangs" are born of the hope that they are part of the revelation of the children of God (Rm 8:22–25).

STUDY QUESTIONS: Do you think Paul sounds arrogant or humble in his appeal to the Galatians to copy him? Should ministers of the gospel maintain a certain distance from their communities? Do we accept prophets who are close to us? Why?

Galatians 4:21–31
SLAVERY OR FREEDOM: WHOSE CHILDREN ARE WE?

²¹ You want to be subject to the Law? Then ²² listen to what the Law says. ·It says, if you remember, that Abraham had two sons, one by the slave girl, and one by his freeborn wife. ²³ The child of the slave girl was born in the ordinary way; the child of the free woman was ²⁴ born as the result of a promise. ·This can be regarded as an allegory: the women stand for the two covenants. The first who comes from Mount Sinai, and whose children are slaves, is ²⁵ Hagar—·since Sinai is in Arabia—and she corresponds to the present Jerusalem that is a ²⁶ slave like her children. ·The Jerusalem above, ²⁷ however, is free and is our mother, ·since scripture says: Shout for joy, you barren women who bore no children! Break into shouts of joy and gladness, you who were never in labor. For there are more sons of the forsaken one ²⁸ than sons of the wedded wife. ·Now you, my brothers, like Isaac, are children of the prom- ²⁹ ise, ·and as at that time the child born in the ordinary way persecuted the child born in the ³⁰ Spirit's way, so also now. ·Does not scripture say: Drive away that slave girl and her son; this slave girl's son is not to share the inherit- ³¹ ance with the son of the free woman? ·So, my brothers, we are the children, not of the slave girl, but of the freeborn wife.

With a third metaphor, this time quoting the law itself, Paul tries to show the temporary role of the law. Previously he showed how the law, like a will, had been mediated and was itself mediator (3:19-20), how it served as guardian (3:23-25, 4:1-7) until the time God appointed for us to become heirs. Now he uses the examples of Abraham's two wives to show the difference in the ways the inheritance was apportioned to their children (4:24-26). Hagar was a slave who was appointed by Sarah at the time of her barrenness to produce an heir for Abraham (Gn 16:1-16). (Such "relative monogamy" reflected acceptable morals for a patriarchal society. The Old Testament is full of examples of ways in which the need to produce a male heir was part of the law and therefore determined sexual morality and laws governing marriage—e.g., Gn 29:31-30:24.) But when Sarah herself produced an heir, even though Hagar's child was the elder, Isaac was designated to bear the promise of Abraham (Gn 21:1-14, 22:15-18).

Geography becomes for Paul a metaphorical method of distinguishing the slave from the free (Ga 4:24-25). Mount Sinai in Arabia and the "present Jerusalem" represent the land of the law and slavery; the "Jerusalem above" (the "new Jerusalem" of Rv 3:12 and 21:2) symbolizes our mother and we are the children of the promise, the free (Ga 4:26-28,31). Christ has already established the

GALATIANS 4:21-31

heavenly Jerusalem and announced the time of the inheritance of the free children. This heavenly Jerusalem is now here in Paul's vision of our redemption (4:26–28).

STUDY QUESTIONS: Are God's covenant and God's promise truly available to all? Paul used the example of Hagar's and Sarah's offspring to convey the differences between slavery and freedom. Can you find some other scriptural or contemporary images to illustrate this difference?

Galatians 5:1 – 6:10
THE ETHICS OF FREEDOM

With Galatians 5, Paul begins the paraenetic, or ethical exhortatory, section of the epistle. It is characteristic of his style, first, to present the theological or doctrinal foundation of Christian life (1:6–4:31) before drawing ethical conclusions (5:1–6:10). This has been called Paul's "indicative-imperative" structure. Paul says, in effect, "In Christ you are a new creation [2 Co 5:17; Ga 6:15]; therefore, let your actions reflect this." Simple pedagogy confirms that Paul's positive approach is more effective than the most consistent admonitions of "You must . . ." and "You must not . . ." in hopes that good actions will produce good people. Yet it is not just a teaching method that Paul propounds. Rather, the Apostle is called to preach the message of justification by the cross of Christ, which now determines all reality (cf. 1 Co 1:17–25). Because Christians have passed from one mode of existence into an entirely different one—that is, from death to life—their actions necessarily reflect the new mode. In other words, this is not so much a mere exhortation to Christians as an elaboration of the clear implications of walking in the newness of life to which they have been called (cf. Rm 6:4). The keynote of this new life as opposed to the slavery of the old is *freedom*.

Galatians 5:1-12
FREEDOM TO BE

5 ¹ When Christ freed us, he meant us to remain free. Stand firm, therefore, and do ² not submit again to the yoke of slavery. ·It is I, Paul, who tell you this: if you allow yourselves to be circumcised, Christ will be of no ³ benefit to you at all. ·With all solemnity I repeat my warning: Everyone who accepts circumcision is obliged to keep the whole Law. ⁴ But if you do look to the Law to make you justified, then you have separated yourselves from Christ, and have fallen from grace. ⁵ Christians are told by the Spirit to look to faith for those rewards that righteousness ⁶ hopes for, ·since in Christ Jesus whether you are circumcised or not makes no difference— what matters is faith that makes its power felt through love.

⁷ You began your race well: who made you ⁸ less anxious to obey the truth? ·You were not ⁹ prompted by him who called you! ·The yeast seems to be spreading through the whole ¹⁰ batch of you. ·I feel sure that, united in the Lord, you will agree with me, and anybody who troubles you in future will be condemned, ¹¹ no matter who he is. ·As for me, my brothers, if I still preach circumcision, why am I still persecuted? If I did that now, would there be ¹² any scandal of the cross? ·Tell those who are disturbing you I would like to see the knife slip.

✠

The opposition between Hagar's and Sarah's sons (4:21-31) has led Paul into a discussion of freedom. Freedom is a Pauline concept as far as the New Testament is concerned (cf. Rm 6:22, 7:6; 1 Co 7:22,39, 9:1,19-23). Nevertheless, it is best understood as the second part of an antithesis that inspired Paul's development of the role of the law as slavery. In other words, freedom for Paul is not the absolute that it is often portrayed in modern descriptions. Indeed, to picture Paul as the champion and patron saint of freedom is to risk misunderstanding him. Paul's world view impelled him to think of humans as serving some spiritual power, whether good or evil. Christ freed us, Paul says, for service—that is, to serve God with our lives. We need to deepen our life in God, clinging firmly to God lest we fall back into slavery (Ga 5:1). The Galatians were tempted to weaken and to submit to the enslaving, and indeed the false, promises of the law, according to Paul, and were being seduced by the agitators' call for circumcision. But, Paul argues, circumcision is the symbol of keeping the "whole law" (Ga 5:3); yet, he points out elsewhere, the law is only fulfilled through love (5:13-15; cf. Rm 13:9-10). But love is threatened by the law which divides. If anyone is circumcised and does not keep the law, he is a hypocrite. And if he must keep the law, then the fulfillment of the promises by

Christ is in vain (cf. Ga 2:15-21). Either choice is an absurd conclusion in the light of the gospel.

Even though Paul describes Christian life in terms of freedom, he applies several qualifiers to this concept. First, freedom is not absolute for Paul; rather, it is freedom from something, for something else. Freedom makes us "obey the truth" (5:7). Freedom cannot bridge the chasm between death and life. The previous state, before faith, was characterized by the law, slavery, death. If Christians do not live in freedom, service to God and the fullness of life, they will slip back into that faithless state (5:4). Paul's strong language about being "separated . . . from Christ" shows the total opposition between the former state and grace. The law cannot "add" to grace; it severs one from the very meaning of grace, which is free gift.

Secondly, freedom is qualified insofar as it does not change a Christian's legal, social or moral obligations. Christians live in the world amid the tensions of everyday life. One of these tensions is the already-but-not-yet character of the life to which they have been called. Although believers have already been justified through Christ, they continue to live with pressures from outside and divisions within Christianity. These are the contexts in which they learn to let their faith "[make] its power felt through love" (5:6). In the course of his writings, Paul opposes the idea that, because they are baptized and so have entered a new life, Christians can withdraw from legitimate obligations in this world, under the pretext of being "free." When Christians in Corinth see faith as a way out of marriage (1 Co

7:1-11), for example, Paul tells them to return to their homes and spouses and to see marriage as a vehicle for giving example to their spouses and for saving themselves. In the same way he upholds the Christian duty to work (see 2 Th 3:6-12) and to pay taxes (Rm 13:6-7). Christians are not to let freedom make them "escape artists" from this world and its reality.

Finally, freedom is qualified both by the responsibility it entails and because of its own incompleteness. Christians are to be leaven in the world, affecting the "whole batch." "Yeast" is an image Paul and the gospel writers (cf. Rm 11:16; 1 Co 5:6; Mt 13:33, 16:6,11,12; Mk 8:15; Lk 12:1, 13:21) find particularly apt to express the effect, for good or evil, that we inevitably have on one another. In Ga 5:9, the leaven is described almost as a cancer. Nevertheless, Paul expresses confidence that his perspective, dictated as it is by the gospel (as opposed to the mere opinion of his adversaries), will win out in the end. Paul is unyielding with the Galatians, fully aware that what he says is not a matter of personal persuasion but the core of the gospel. Freedom for him involves his responsibility to bring others to the truth.

But the fullness of freedom is not yet possessed by Christians. They have begun the race well, Paul says (5:7), yet now it looks as if they are losing. ("Running a race" is another favorite Pauline image —cf. 1 Co 9:24,26; Ph 2:16; 2 Tm 4:7). Freedom is part of the new way of life, a journey that, once undertaken, needs to be completed. The truth of Christian freedom is only achieved in ultimate, total union with the Lord, a union only partially experienced now.

If Paul's meaning in 5:11 seems rather vague, the following verse is shockingly clear! The first can probably best be understood as a further example of Paul's saying that each person "should continue as he was when God's call reached him" (1 Co 7:17). To the Jews, Paul preaches circumcision (cf. 9:19-23). But he fought desperately against the circumcision of the pagans. Nevertheless, even after the compromise at Jerusalem (Ac 15:19-29), Paul had Timothy circumcised (16:1-3), probably because he views this as a way of having Timothy be more readily accepted by the Jewish-Christian authorities. And so Paul may have left himself open to the charge of inconsistency, the very accusation he seemed to levy against Cephas (cf. Ga 2:11-14). Yet simple consistency is not his point. Something far greater is at issue in his debate with Cephas, namely grace, expressed in the form of the full inclusion of the pagans into the community. The freedom of the gospel is a scandal for those who cannot accept that sinners are justified through grace, not through merit. Ga 5:12 is perhaps less startling when seen in the light of the way eunuchs were thought of in Paul's day, especially by the Jews. With characteristic sarcasm (as contrasted with real malice), the Apostle may have been mocking the agitators who preached circumcision among the pagans. Eunuchs were fairly common among the Greeks, especially in the temples of certain goddesses. Perhaps Paul was saying that in their efforts to make Jews of the pagan converts, the agitators, with a slip of the knife, risk confirming them as pagans by performing not a circumcision but a castration! Paul's comment, then, is perhaps redeemed by humor.

STUDY QUESTIONS: Do you agree with Paul that it is possible to be free from sin and released from the kind of slavery Paul refers to? What are the boundaries to our freedom? Can a person be free if he or she is imprisoned? Why? Paul emphasized the importance of faith in Christ as having a higher priority than following the law. What then does he mean by his warning about falling from grace?

Galatians 5:13–26
FREEDOM TO LOVE

13 My brothers, you were called, as you know, to liberty; but be careful, or this liberty will provide an opening for self-indulgence. Serve
14 one another, rather, in works of love, ·since the whole of the Law is summarized in a single command: Love your neighbor as yourself.
15 If you go snapping at each other and tearing each other to pieces, you had better watch or you will destroy the whole community.
16 Let me put it like this: if you are guided by the Spirit you will be in no danger of yielding
17 to self-indulgence, ·since self-indulgence is the opposite of the Spirit, the Spirit is totally against such a thing, and it is precisely because the two are so opposed that you do not always
18 carry out your good intentions. ·If you are led
19 by the Spirit, no law can touch you. ·When self-indulgence is at work the results are obvious: fornication, gross indecency and sexual
20 irresponsibility; ·idolatry and sorcery; feuds and wrangling, jealousy, bad temper and quar-
21 rels; disagreements, factions, ·envy; drunkenness, orgies and similar things. I warn you now, as I warned you before: those who behave like this will not inherit the kingdom of
22 God. ·What the Spirit brings is very different: love, joy, peace, patience, kindness, goodness,
23 trustfulness, ·gentleness and self-control. There can be no law against things like that, of
24 course. ·You cannot belong to Christ Jesus

unless you crucify all self-indulgent passions and desires.

²⁵ Since the Spirit is our life, let us be directed
²⁶ by the Spirit. ·We must stop being conceited, provocative and envious.

☦

Paul returns in 5:13 to the concept of freedom (5:1). Taken as an absolute, freedom could degenerate easily again into the slavery of self-indulgence. Paul, who likes antitheses, evokes the opposition between the spirit and self-indulgence to emphasize that freedom *from* sin must be expressed as freedom *for* service (5:17; cf. Rm 8:1–11, where a similar opposition is expressed in terms of our spiritual and unspiritual selves; cf. 1 Co 2:10–3:4). Love is the antidote for the slavery of self-indulgence (that is, the turned inward, self-seeking, egotistical, sinful part of our nature). Paul sums up the meaning of love in the phrase "Serve one another" (Ga 5:13). The Spirit of God that has been "poured into our hearts" (Rm 5:5) is the spirit of love and unity, enabling Christians to sincerely be good to one another (12:9–10). Self-indulgence represents for Paul all that is contrary to the Spirit of God; the kinds of self-indulgence enumerated in Ga 5:19–21 are the fleshly expressions that alienate members of the community from one another. The crux of the matter is summed up in 5:14–15—the "whole of the Law" is contained in the single command, "Love your neighbor as yourself" (cf. Lv 19:18; Rm 13:9–10). When this absolute law of love is compromised—whether by the extreme of legalism or licentiousness—the whole community, which is itself the great testimony of faith in the gospel, is threatened. This explains Paul's urgent insistence in Ga 5:15. Far from being a reductionist, he identifies love as the pulse of Christianity, as the measure of faith-life.

Paul uses the opposition between self-indulgence and spirit to describe the antithetical, mutually exclusive principles of motivation. Self-indulgence is an expression of selfishness destructive of love. The spirit, on the other hand, refers to the other-directed virtues that nourish community, making it possible for those with gifts to share with those in need (cf. 1 Co 12:12–21). Law, which by definition can govern only what is permissible or not and whatever can be measured, cannot limit the positive, life-giving, continually growing fruits of the Spirit of God. (The translators of *The Jerusalem Bible* do well to consistently capitalize "Spirit" each time it appears in Ga 5:16–26, since it is difficult if not impossible to determine to what extent Paul envisioned qualifying differences between the divine and the human spirits.)

Finally, a word about the phrase "kingdom of God" in 5:21 is needed. Although this phrase does occur in Paul (e.g., Rm 14:17; 1 Co 4:20, 6:9,10, 15:24,50; 2 Th 1:5) in contexts which suggest its importance in the original Christian gospel, the phrase is more commonly associated with the synoptics, referring to God's coming eschatological reign (Mt 12:28, 21:43; Mk 1:15, 4:11, 9:1; Lk 4:43, 9:62; and passim). Paul seems to prefer to speak about the *present* reign of *Christ,* which is growing and becoming ever more inclusive until Christ becomes all in all and restores the world to God (1 Co 15:24–28). The allusion to God's kingdom in Ga 5:21 might suggest that Paul is drawing on a pre-Pauline Christian tradition, preserved in baptismal and eucharistic texts by the early Christians. These sacramental contexts could have provided him a way of describing the opposition between life outside and inside the church, the contrast between the time before and the time after faith.

STUDY QUESTIONS: How can a person be certain of following the guidance of the Holy Spirit? What does it mean to do the loving thing? What does Paul mean by liberty? What is its relation to love?

Galatians 6:1–10
LIFE IN COMMUNITY

6 ¹ Brothers, if one of you misbehaves, the more spiritual of you who set him right should do so in a spirit of gentleness, not forgetting that you may be tempted yourselves. ² You should carry each other's troubles and ³ fulfill the law of Christ. ·It is the people who are not important who often make the mistake ⁴ of thinking that they are. ·Let each of you examine his own conduct: if you find anything to boast about, it will at least be something of your own, not just something better than your ⁵ neighbor has. ·Everyone has his own burden to carry.

⁶ People under instruction should always contribute something to the support of the man who is instructing them.

⁷ Don't delude yourself into thinking God can be cheated: where a man sows, there he ⁸ reaps: ·if he sows in the field of self-indulgence he will get a harvest of corruption out of it; if he sows in the field of the Spirit he will get ⁹ from it a harvest of eternal life. ·We must never get tired of doing good because if we don't give up the struggle we shall get our har- ¹⁰ vest at the proper time. ·While we have the chance, we must do good to all, and especially to our brothers in the faith.

✠

Throughout the ethical part (5:1-6:10) of this epistle, Paul describes life in the community, life together after Baptism. In the beginning of this part he was concerned with agitators for the law from the outside (5:1-12) and with tensions within the community (5:13-26). In 6:1 he turns to the question of forgiveness and fraternal correction (cf. Mt 18:15-18). Unconditional love, Paul implies, is expressed in unlimited forgiveness, concern for others and mutual encouragement and guidance. Guided by a spirit of gentleness, members of the gospel community support, admonish, challenge one another. The measure of growth in love is the ability to forgive and to become more inclusive, thus eliminating any barriers to forgiveness. Paul seems to be reflecting on implications of Jesus' answer to Peter's question about how many times another Christian should be forgiven (Mt 18:21-22). The authority of the church gives expression to the gospel in the forgiveness of sins.

This is the essence of the love command that spells out the law of Christ (Rm 8:1-3) and reveals the unfulfilled purpose of the Old Testament law (see especially Ga 3:19-22, 5:13-14). For Paul, Christ did not abolish the law as such but brought it to the completion which we could not ourselves accomplish. Paul does not deny that the law was good (cf. Rm 7:12) but that it had the power to save. The law could have no other fulfillment than love.

Attaining this fulfillment is possible only through Christ. When Jesus offered himself, becoming obedient, even taking the form of a slave (Ph 2:7), submitting to death on the cross (2:8), he gave us more than an example. Christ gave us the *power* to love one another (Ga 5:13) and so to make of our whole lives an offering to God (Rm 12:1). This is the challenge of community worthy of the name Christian (cf. Ga 2:19–21; 2 Co 5:13–15).

For the early Christians, Jesus' words replaced the law. Although Paul apparently never met Jesus during the course of his lifetime, tradition preserved Jesus' preaching and Paul sometimes reveals his direct contact with and reliance on the authority of this preaching (e.g., 1 Co 7:10–11, 11:23–25). The teaching of Jesus that a preacher deserves his keep (cf. Mt 10:10; 1 Co 9:14) probably inspired Paul's admonition in Ga 6:6. Paul personally rejects benefits for himself from the principle of this dictum. Apparently this is because he does not want to risk giving reason for any additional protest his detractors could use against him in accusing him of personal gain resulting from his ministry (1 Co 9:15; 2 Co 11:7–9). Furthermore, the creative, realistic Paul probably found additional opportunity as well as material for his teaching by working with his hands among the common folk. Meeting them as an equal on their own working grounds and plying his own tent-making trade for a living (Ac 18:1–4, 20:33–35; 1 Co 4:12), Paul was able to give more credible witness. The gospel is understood not only in what the Apostle said, but also in what he did.

And not only is the gospel in what he did, but in the way he did it.

Undoubtedly having his own profession added concrete images to Paul's gospel preaching. Paul reflects in Ga 6:7–10 Jesus' own imagery of the harvest, an image Jesus most often used to speak of the judgment of the world (cf. Mt 13:30,39; Mk 4:29; Jn 4:35–38). In addition, Paul was probably inspired with concrete images by his workingman's status. His own need to earn his living effectively prevented his preaching from becoming too heady, ephemeral, out of touch. Paul applies a simple principle that says we sow what we reap; a great harvest can be expected from patient, hopeful, diligent sowing. Even self-indulgence reaps its own product, corruption. But the tireless struggle of sowing well will reap the harvest of eternal life. We must do good to all. Yet it is especially members of our own community of faith that have a priority on our labors of love (6:10), as together we wait expectantly for the eternal harvest.

STUDY QUESTIONS: How does freedom relate to communal love? What are the limits to love? Is it possible, really, to constantly accept others completely, without resentment? Why?

Galatians 6:11–18
A POSTSCRIPT FOR EMPHASIS

¹¹ Take good note of what I am adding in my
¹² own handwriting and in large letters. ·It is only self-interest that makes them want to force circumcision on you—they want to escape per-
¹³ secution for the cross of Christ—·they accept circumcision but do not keep the Law themselves; they only want you to be circumcised
¹⁴ so that they can boast of the fact. ·As for me, the only thing I can boast about is the cross of our Lord Jesus Christ, through whom the world is crucified to me, and I to the world.
¹⁵ It does not matter if a person is circumcised or not; what matters is for him to become an alto-
¹⁶ gether new creature. ·Peace and mercy to all who follow this rule, who form the Israel of God.
¹⁷ I want no more trouble from anybody after this; the marks on my body are those of Jesus.
¹⁸ The grace of our Lord Jesus Christ be with your spirit, my brothers. Amen.

✠

To give emphasis to this letter, Paul adds a postscript recapitulating his warning in terms that indicate his personal agony over the Galatians. The charge he lays against the agitators is that they are hypocrites. They try to escape persecution through externals, and they are neither true to the law nor to the cross. They are only using the number of Galatian circumcisions for their own advantage (6:13). The phrase "persecution for the cross of Christ" (6:12) probably refers to some form of alienation from those outside the community (e.g., from mainstream Judaism, as Paul once persecuted Christians). And perhaps even more painful for these early Christians is the fact that Paul's phrase probably conveys something of their own deep confusion and doubt because of the mockery and outright rejection they encounter as a result of their faith in a crucified Lord. As the focus of faith, the cross is a stumbling block to Jews, folly to pagans and undoubtedly a sign of contradiction even for believers (cf. 6:15; 1 Co 1:17–23).

From the point of view of the gospel, circumcision is indifferent (Ga 6:15; 1 Co 7:19). The danger in even considering circumcision is that it would be assigned value even after the message of the cross, which caused a reevaluation of everything. With the coming of the reign of Christ, Christians must not be distracted by any such requirements of the law. All that is essential is that each Christian becomes a "new creature" (Ga 6:15; cf. 2 Co 5:17), a member of the new community of Jews and pagans who together, through Christ, are refashioned into the "Israel of God" (Ga 6:16). It is as if Paul hits upon the phrase that says it all: the church is the Israel of God, a new creation. Part of the newness is the collective, community dimension of our common identity in faith.

Finally, Paul says in almost menacing tones, he

GALATIANS 6:11–18

wants no more trouble (6:17). He will not argue further. His own body speaks eloquently of the trials he has endured for the gospel. He bears the marks of Jesus, and by speaking of these he tries to silence his detractors. Paul probably refers to the fact that in his flesh he has suffered for the community (cf. 2 Co 11:23–29; Ph 3:10; Col 1:24; 2 Tm 3:11), which is the body of Christ (cf. Rm 12:4–5; 1 Co 12:12–30). The epistle to the Galatians concludes abruptly, just as it began. If God's grace is with them, Christians have no further need of anything. Amen.

STUDY QUESTIONS: Discuss some of the ways each of us actually experiences new life or becomes a "new creature" (6:15). Is the idea of a "new creature" for Paul an individual or a community idea? Both? Why?

The Letter of Paul to the Church in Rome

Romans, the longest of Paul's epistles, is clearly one of his most important. In this letter, Paul lays out his basic theological tenets which he calls the "Good News," that is, the gospel (1:1,9,16, 16:25; cf. Ga 1:6–9). Unlike Paul's other letters, Romans does not appear to be one side of a written conversation which requires a hypothetical filling in of gaps in order to reconstruct the whole. Although written in letter form, Romans is more properly a stylized epistle in which the main body containing Paul's message reads like a treatise rather than like the more familiar dialogue typical of a letter. Paul does not really provide in Romans many clues as to why he addresses certain problems or why he even undertook the task of writing to this community which he did not yet know personally (Rm 1:9–15, 15:22–33). Yet the very fact that Paul is a certain distance from the Christian community at Rome probably accounts for the uncharacteristic objectivity and clarity with which he sets out to explain the gospel basics.

Little can be known for certain about why Paul wrote this epistle from the information he himself provides, so interpreters have proposed a variety of explanations. Since several seem to be plausible, it might be better not to single out any particular one as the only acceptable explanation. Rather, three prominent explanations seem to round out the picture and help us understand Paul's multiple reasons for writing and clarify the message of Romans itself.

First, Romans serves as a kind of introduction of Paul himself and of the gospel he preaches to the Roman community. As such, this epistle helps prepare the way for Paul's projected visit to Rome (1:9–13, 15:22–33). This explanation aids our understanding of an apparent contradiction in the fact that Paul writes to Rome even though he himself says in 15:20 that he does not "wish to build on other men's foundations." Tradition holds that the Christian community in Rome was founded by Peter, and Paul's own words verify the fact that Christianity was already well-established there by the time Paul wrote Romans (around A.D. 57 or 58). Paul, who writes letters to other communities to encourage and correct them and to answer their questions, denies that he has any doubts about the Romans (15:14). On the contrary. Their faith, he says, "is spoken of all over the world" (1:8). Yet it stands to reason that Rome, capital of the world and springboard for Paul's projected goal of Spain (15:24,28), would be an obvious exception to the principle Paul personally espouses in 15:20. The community at Rome would be a powerfully important and influential one. Paul's reputation would have preceded him wherever he went. He would understandably have been concerned about misconceptions regarding the gospel he preached. These plagued him even in communities which he himself founded and knew well, such as those in Galatia and Corinth. Paul wanted to prevent anything that would have hampered the gospel's acceptance either in Rome or Spain or in any other place he planned to visit. Thus, in view of his proposed journey, it is reasonable that he would outline as clearly as possible the main teachings of the gospel he preaches.

Secondly, Romans serves as a kind of summation of Paul's theological perspective, a testament he leaves as a legacy to the early Christian communities and to the church in our day. Of course, Paul himself probably did not realize that Romans would be one of the last letters he would write, so he did not make a conscious attempt to include all that he might have wanted to include in a kind of a will. Yet in Romans we have the most systematic of Paul's writings, and the relative objectivity of Paul's position vis-à-vis the Roman community enhances the clarity of the message. The Apostle himself may also have realized the merits of writing down and circulating the gospel basics, for it seems he added a kind of cover letter (Romans 16) to the first fifteen chapters and apparently sent this copy of Romans to the church at Ephesus with his emissary and friend Phoebe (16:1–2). The original, consisting of Rm 1:1–15:33, he sent to Rome (see the discussion of this hypothesis regarding Romans 16, p. 274).

Finally, Paul provides in Romans a model pastoral letter for a mixed community composed of both former Jews and pagans. Although there is some risk in trying to conclude too much about the exact nature of the community at Rome from the meager information Paul furnishes (14:1–15:33), much of the message of this epistle makes better sense in the light of the multiple potential problems that would have been experienced by a mixed community. Historical evidence does bring to light some facts that could have bearing on the particular situation of the Christian community in Rome at the time Paul wrote. In A.D. 49, Emperor Claudius expelled the Jews from Rome because, the historian Suetonius tells us, there was a disturbance among them regarding "Chrestus" (cf. Ac 18:2). This is generally assumed to be a reference to Christ. Many Jews probably returned to Rome after Claudius' death in A.D. 53 or 54, but those who had also become Christian would have returned to find that a very pagan-oriented version of Christianity had developed in the absence of Jewish influence during those formative years. In the main, the Jews who lived in Rome in the first place would have been brought there as slaves or at least subordinates to Roman (i.e., pagan) masters. In Rome, Jews would have been a minority, and Jewish Christians would have been a minority within a minority. In the short period of four to five years when the Jews were in forced exile from Rome, the pagan interpretation of Christianity would have gained strength, and the returning Jewish Christians might have had difficulty adapting to a religion they hardly recognized. The key for this interpretation is provided, according to its proponents, by the phrase Paul coins for use in Romans, "the obedience of faith" (1:5, 16:26). In short, the Jewish Christians, interested in preserving emphasis on *obedience* to God's will which they formerly believed to be revealed in the law, would have been dismayed upon their return to Rome to find a Christianity that so emphasized freedom from the law because it was dominated by a non-Jewish perspective. They would have had a hard time identifying with the law-free interpretation so foreign to their own roots. On the other hand, the pagan Christians in Rome experienced Christianity apart from the law and even, for a few years, apart from the influence of the Jewish Christians, and they might have so stressed the freedom of faith that they evidenced some feelings of superiority regarding the returning, more law-bound Jewish Christians. Thus Paul invokes the phrase "obedience of faith" as the object of the gospel that acts as a mutual corrective for both Jewish and pagan Christians. Romans, in this view, is a development of the gospel as God's power to save and to reconcile both Jews and pagans (cf. the theme of Romans in 1:16–17). Since *all* have sinned and are equally alienated from God, Paul insists, *all*, Jews and pagans alike, need to obey God's will through faith in Jesus Christ.

Romans, then, can be considered as introduction to Paul and to his gospel, a kind of theological legacy Paul left to Christianity and a model pastoral directive to a mixed community. These three explanations provide a composite picture telling why Paul wrote this letter. They also furnish important insights into the structure of Romans and the theology Paul develops there.

The structure of Romans is relatively clear and simple. After a brief introduction consisting of address, greeting and thanksgiving (1:1–15), Paul expresses (1:16–17) the theme of the letter thus:

> ... it [i.e., the Good News, the gospel] is the power of God saving all who have faith—Jews first, but Greeks as well—since this is what reveals the justice of God to us: it shows how faith leads to faith, or as scripture says: The upright man finds life through faith.

Then follows the doctrinal part of the letter in 1:18–8:39. Here Paul shows that all needed the salvation he announced in the theme. This salvation is revealed in the gospel. He shows this need by saying that all have sinned (1:18–3:20). He then uses Abraham as an example that all are saved through faith rather than by works of the law (4:1–25). Paul concludes this doctrinal section with a description of Christian life (5:1–8:39). Romans 9–11 represent a kind of parenthesis which probably can be included in the doctrinal part of the epistle, but with their well-defined introduction (9:1–5) and conclusion (11:33–36), these three chapters seem to be a rather self-contained treatment of the question of God's fidelity in view of the Jewish rejection of the gospel. The final section, 12:1–16:27, contains the ethical applications and exhortations which are Paul's pastoral conclusions to the statements of faith he made in 1:1–8:39.

Romans, one of the last letters Paul wrote, as noted above, was probably composed around A.D. 57 or 58, perhaps at Corinth, although the date and place of writing are uncertain. From the contents, it is reasonable to conclude that the community Paul addressed was a mixed one of Jewish and pagan Christians who struggled with doctrinal and ethical obstacles to their unity. Paul's relatively systematic and objective approach makes Romans an appropriate model for today's church.

Romans 1:1–7
PAUL, A MISSIONARY WITH A MESSAGE

1 ¹ From Paul, a servant of Christ Jesus who has been called to be an apostle, and specially chosen to preach the Good News that ² God ·promised long ago through his prophets in the scriptures.

³ This news is about the Son of God who, according to the human nature he took, was a ⁴ descendant of David: ·it is about Jesus Christ our Lord who, in the order of the spirit, the spirit of holiness that was in him, was proclaimed Son of God in all his power through ⁵ his resurrection from the dead. ·Through him we received grace and our apostolic mission to preach the obedience of faith to all pagan na- ⁶ tions in honor of his name. ·You are one of these nations, and by his call belong to Jesus ⁷ Christ. ·To you all, then, who are God's beloved in Rome, called to be saints, may God our Father and the Lord Jesus Christ send grace and peace.

✠

According to the traditional ancient form of a letter, Paul begins with his name and a greeting, drawing together some of his favorite theological terms of identity (1:1–2). He then proceeds to the content of his message (1:3-5) and to specify those to whom he addresses this, one of the most important of his writings (1:6-7). Paul does not waste words, yet his introduction of himself and his gospel provides a rich prelude to the ideas he intends to develop in sixteen chapters. Paul's caring, sensitive address to the Roman community is ample evidence of his pastoral preoccupations. Yet, reassuring though Paul's initial words are, they are not to be taken lightly. They set the weighty, almost urgent tone of the epistle. The Apostle crowds enough into the first sentence to grip the readers and compel their attention.

Paul describes himself first of all as a servant (1:1), a title he favors because it signifies absolute commitment to the Lord (cf. Ga 1:10; Ph 1:1; Tt 1:1). In the Epistle to the Philippians, Christ himself is described as the example par excellence of the humble, obedient slave (Ph 2:5-11). Isaiah, the prophet most frequently quoted by Paul, provides inspiration for this conception of Christ's and of the Apostle's own role in God's plan of salvation. Especially in his identity as Apostle to the pagans, Paul drew on Isaiah's conception of the servant of God who would be a "light of the nations" (Is 42:1-7, 49:6).

Paul further describes himself as an apostle, "specially chosen" for preaching the Good News. Paul had been a Pharisee (Ph 3:5) and the Pharisees' own name meant "separated ones," those whose piety and zeal for the Jewish law distinguished them even from other Jews. The Pharisees became dominant as first-century Judaism was increasingly marked by tensions and divisions. Perhaps in opposition to the Pharisaic separatism that characterized his former life in Judaism, Paul presents a kind of new understanding of the purpose of being chosen or distinguished by God's will (cf. Ga 1:15–16). He was given his apostolic role so that he could serve God by bringing the pagan nations to honor God's name (Rm 1:5). Like the Christian community itself, the Apostle is chosen for others; he does not represent any special interests, but rather is sent to the pagans to illustrate the universality of the gospel. Paul's purpose is to preach the Good News (1:1), that is, the "obedience of faith" (1:5, 16:26). This phrase Paul coins in Romans to use as a challenge to the mixed community there. The Apostle is empowered by the Good News he himself hears and is compelled to preach (1 Co 9:16; cf. 2 Co 5:14). Paul's success is not measured by the numbers he baptized (1 Co 1:14–17), but by his preaching to the pagans who represent the universal mission field of the gospel.

The "Good News" is another term for the gospel Paul preaches. It is "news" in that it is faith's identification of Jesus as the promised Son of God (cf. Rm 1:2–3). It is "good" in the sense that it proclaims grace and peace for all who are called to the faith (1:6–7). The gospel Paul preaches is not mere history or biography, but the power of God (1:16). The four Gospels we know do have a story line that follows Jesus from his early ministry of miracles and powerful sayings in Galilee to his death on the cross in Jerusalem. The composition of these Gospels, between about A.D. 65 and 100, came after Paul's preaching and writing which was done about A.D. 49–60. So Paul was the first presenter of the gospel. For him, the gospel is revealed as God's power to save sinners. This free, saving power is what makes God's news "good."

The gospel was promised beforehand by the prophets in the scriptures (1:2). Humankind, under the burden of sin and death, could not free itself. Salvation was first held out as a promise and then fulfilled in Christ. In a sense, the gospel follows a natural line of progression; it is the fulfillment of the Old Testament (cf. 3:21,31). All of the Old Testament, including the law, is "prophetic" in the sense that it all points to its own completion in the gospel of Jesus.

The gospel is "about" God's Son; the content is Jesus (1:3-4). The Incarnation is at the heart of the Good News. Nevertheless, references to Jesus' earthly life are scant in Paul. His starting point is the Resurrection (1 Co 15:3-8). The Resurrection is the saving event and thus it becomes the focal point through which Paul portrays every other significant event of the human story: sin, suffering, death, salvation, life itself. In order to underscore the reality of the Resurrection as the power of salvation, Paul works backward, as it were, from the Resurrection to the saving effect of Jesus' death on sinful humanity. Jesus really died and was buried. This means that he was truly human. As a human, he was born, he descended from a traceable ancestry, the line of David (1:3). David is not only Jesus' human ancestor, but Jesus' theological father as well. Like Abraham (cf. 4:1-25; Ga 3:15-18), David holds a positive place in Paul's presentation of the history of salvation, whereas Adam and Moses, as bearers of sin and the law, have a negative significance for Paul.

"In the order of the Spirit," Jesus is proclaimed Son of God (Rm 1:4). Having died in obedience to the Father, Jesus was raised up by God to become the "eldest of many" (8:29). His Resurrection was a promise for us. According to Paul, the Good News is based on the fact that God raised Jesus from the dead and so Jesus is Lord (10:9). "Lord" is Paul's most frequently used title for Jesus. With faith in Jesus as Lord, we are able, with Paul, to address God as "Father" (cf. 8:15; Ga 4:6–7).

Through the person and the redemptive action of Jesus, Paul says, we have received apostleship and grace (Rm 1:5). The collective "we" refers to membership in a community established in authority (apostleship) and faith (grace). The purpose of Paul's own mission is to effect the pagans' obedience of faith (1:5, 16:26). The Jewish-Christian minority in Rome might have tended to overemphasize the necessity of obedience. The pagan Christians would have been more tempted to stress the freedom implied in faith to the point of complacency. Paul provides a mutual corrector, saying that in obedience to God and faith in Jesus, all are called to be saints (1:7).

STUDY QUESTIONS: In what ways do we describe ourselves as Christians? How is the gospel "good news" for our world? What is meant by preaching the "obedience of faith" (1:5)?

Romans 1:8–15
PAUL'S SPIRITUAL WORSHIP: PREACHING THE GOSPEL

⁸ First I thank my God through Jesus Christ for all of you and for the way in which your ⁹ faith is spoken of all over the world. ·The God I worship spiritually by preaching the Good News of his Son knows that I never fail to ¹⁰ mention you in my prayers, ·and to ask to be allowed at long last the opportunity to visit ¹¹ you, if he so wills. ·For I am longing to see you either to strengthen you by sharing a spir- ¹² itual gift with you, ·or what is better, to find encouragement among you from our common ¹³ faith. ·I want you to know, brothers, that I have often planned to visit you—though until now I have always been prevented—in the hope that I might work as fruitfully among you as ¹⁴ I have done among the other pagans. ·I owe a duty to Greeks just as much as to barbarians, to the educated just as much as to the unedu- ¹⁵ cated, ·and it is this that makes me want to bring the Good News to you too in Rome.

✠

A thanksgiving, like a greeting, is part of the ancient opening form of a letter. The thanksgiving and prayer in 1:8–15 reveals the warmth of the Apostle's pastoral heart. They do not express the sentiments *expected* of an authority, least of all of the tyrannical egomaniac Paul is sometimes falsely accused of being. Rather, these verses voice the longings of a lover, a person brimming with passionate enthusiasm (which literally means "God-filled"). Paul worships God spiritually (1:9) by preaching the gospel. He accepts a worldwide mission which knows no social, political, religious or geographical boundaries. Deep conviction formed by experience causes Paul to acknowledge that in his ministry he is not only giver but receiver (1:11-12). The language of faith is one that is shared, listened to *and* spoken.

And the sharing of gifts is not merely either material or spiritual, but both. Paul's physical presence with the Romans would itself be a blessing for both (1:11). Toward the end of this letter Paul will more fully describe the significance of a Christian's sharing of material goods symbolized by the collection (15:25-29), but in Romans 1 he prays that the encouragement Christians can gain by the sharing of common faith will be the fruit of a visit to Rome which he hopes is part of God's will (1:10-13). The God of Paul's understanding is not indifferent to the basic human need of friends' enjoying being together, being good to one another, sharing hospitality. In fact, just as the Incarnation is at the heart of the Christian message (1:3), Christians' material support and love for each other is essential to the gospel's being preached (1:11-15).

Later in this epistle, Paul will say, "Avoid getting into debt, except the debt of mutual love" (13:8). Here in 1:14 he also describes a debt he himself owes to Greeks and barbarians, to the educated and the uneducated—i.e., to everyone (1:14). This debt is the debt of love, one incurred when he himself was seized by Christ (cf. Ph 3:12). The preaching of the gospel has a certain urgency about it—the Apostle cannot rest until he has taken it to the ends of the known world, that is, to Spain via Rome (Rm 15:24,28).

STUDY QUESTIONS: What does Paul mean when he says he wants to share "a spiritual gift" with the Romans (1:11)? For us to have common faith, on what must there be agreement? What makes Paul "owe a duty" (1:14)?

Romans 1:16–8:39
PAUL'S GOSPEL:—A DOCTRINE WHICH IS POWER

Rm 1:16–17 spells out the theme of Paul's epistles and 1:18–8:39 goes on to develop the implications of his theme. Paul shows in this doctrinal part of Romans that all have sinned and that, therefore, all need the justification effected by the Good News. The Apostle insists repeatedly that the way to salvation has already begun (cf. 5:1–11, 8:1–39), so that sin no longer has dominion over us (5:12–21, 6:1–7:25).

Important characteristic features of Paul's theology appear throughout this doctrinal section (1:18–8:39). For instance, Paul's emphasis on the fact that salvation has already begun is part of his faith-vision which focuses on what Christ has done for us. Only after Paul states that the gospel is the power of God for universal salvation (1:16–17) does the Apostle demonstrate human powerlessness under sin (1:18–3:20, 5:12–21, 7:1–25) that necessitated Christ's free gift of justification (5:1–11). Further, throughout Romans, as throughout Paul's other writings, there exists a strong tension between the already-now and the not-yet poles of Christian experience. That is, we find in Paul a pull between his accent on the new life of freedom from sin effected through Baptism (6:1–11) and the former life of sin that continues to tug at the Christian's commitment to God through Christ (7:1–25).

The fact that sin is universal can be demonstrated. In Romans, Paul proceeds with three demonstrations of this fact. First, he shows that all people, Jews as well as pagans, have sinned (1:18–3:31). Secondly, the Apostle recalls that since the time of Adam, all have sinned (5:12–21). Thirdly, speaking in the first person, Paul describes the experience of sin that every person can identify with (7:1–25). Yet, despite the inexorable fact of sin affecting all people, Paul intersperses his three demonstrations of sin's universality with cogent reflections on the accessibility of justification through faith for all. After announcing this accessibility by God's power in 1:16–17, Paul points to the example of Abraham (4:1–25), the saving effects of Baptism (6:1–23) and the Christian experience of freedom from condemnation (5:1–11, 8:1–39).

Romans 1:16–17
THE THEME OF ROMANS: THE GOSPEL IS GOD'S POWER TO SAVE ALL

16 For I am not ashamed of the Good News:
it is the power of God saving all who have
17 faith—Jews first, but Greeks as well—since
this is what reveals the justice of God to us:
it shows how faith leads to faith, or as scripture says: The upright man finds life through faith.

✠

The Apostle Paul is not ashamed of the Good News. It is the power of salvation (1:16). The Good News —the gospel—is freedom from fear and from self-serving. The proud, boastful person may be overly defensive for fear of being ashamed, but not Paul. There is a lot of fear underlying pride since it is always possible to lose what one is proud of, but this is not so with faith, which focuses not on what we possess but on the fidelity of God. Paul's authority and his preaching come not from him but from God. The gospel completely determines the Apostle's point of view. In fact, the gospel identifies the Apostle, grounds his authority, constitutes his message as God's power (1:5). Totally reliant on God, then, the Apostle preaches shamelessly, by word and deed, the message of salvation (cf. 15:18–19).

The power of the gospel is manifest in the justification of all the faithful which it effects. Paul focuses on justification as an expression of the justice of God. The law and the prophets of the Old Testament revealed a concept of God's justice that could be reflected in human society, but was dramatically different from human constructs of justice. God's ways are not our ways (Is 55:8–9). Thus we must be converted to submit to the revelation of God's ways. The purpose of governments and courts in ancient Israel, the "divine right" of the king, was to be a representative of God, to insure the protection of the defenseless and of those who have no rights. These are personified in the widows and children. In other words, God acts through authority in order to defend the defenseless, to bring justice in the form of gratuitous mercy.

Throughout the Old Testament, the godly person is described as the one who seeks justice. God's just will as revealed in the law and obedience to the law is justification, according to the Old Testament. But Judaism, by the time of Jesus and Paul, came to be reduced to a system that defined justification too narrowly. Sinners (i.e., pagans, unrighteous Jews), who did not obey the law according to this understanding of it, were considered excluded from justification. Paul, however, represents justification as the initial moment of salvation. According to the Apostle, sinners are included as justified because justification is not merited but attained through faith (Rm 1:17). Faith is the free gift of grace, accessible to all—Jews first, and then to Greeks as well. God's saving message put simply is this: God's justice is mercy; faith that this is so is salvation.

The starting point for understanding the truth of the gospel is not intellectual assent but faith—that is, the wholehearted embrace of the experience of being saved without *deserving* to be. The gospel is not a catechism, nor is it familiarity with the events recorded in the scriptures. One does not read, memorize or recite the gospel. The gospel may be experienced without knowing many facts about Jesus. Conversely, many objective facts can be known about Jesus and about Christianity without there being any experience of gospel. The impact of the gospel is the *power* to convert a person's vision so that mercy is seen as justice and vice versa. In this vision is the opportunity Paul calls "justification."

STUDY QUESTIONS: Paul says the Good News is the power of God saving all who have faith. What does it mean to have faith? What is an "upright" person?

Romans 1:18 – 4:25
THE NEED FOR JUSTIFICATION THROUGH FAITH IS UNIVERSAL

God has given all the power of justification in the gospel, Paul announced in the thesis statement of 1:16–17. In 1:18–3:31, the Apostle provides his first demonstration of the universal need for this power to be given, since no one can achieve it, for all have sinned (cf. 5:12–21, 7:1–25). The ancient world, no less than our own, tended to divide people into two camps of "we" and "they"; for the Greeks, there were Greeks and barbarians. The Jews identified themselves as the chosen people, distinct from the pagans (also called the "Gentiles" or "nations") who were considered sinners by the Jews' definition (i.e., they were outside the justice of the law). Paul uses the language familiar to his readers. He shows the sinfulness of all by showing the sinfulness of these two groups. First he reviews the obvious, identifying the pagans as sinners (1:18–32). Then he will turn to the Jews (2:1–3:20), appealing to the sacred scriptures themselves to substantiate the truth of his claim about the sinfulness of the chosen people (3:10–20). When he has done this, he recapitulates (3:21–31), in modified terms, the thesis of 1:16–17: "The justice of God . . . comes through faith to everyone, Jew and pagan alike" (3:22). Finally, he uses the example of Abraham (4:1–25) to show that justification comes through faith rather than through the law.

Romans 1:18–32
THE TESTIMONY:
THE PAGANS HAVE SINNED

¹⁸ The anger of God is being revealed from heaven against all the impiety and depravity of men who keep truth imprisoned in their ¹⁹ wickedness. ·For what can be known about God is perfectly plain to them since God him- ²⁰ self has made it plain. ·Ever since God created the world his everlasting power and deity— however invisible—have been there for the mind to see in the things he has made. That is ²¹ why such people are without excuse: ·they knew God and yet refused to honor him as God or to thank him; instead, they made nonsense out of logic and their empty minds were ²² darkened. ·The more they called themselves philosophers, the more stupid they grew, ²³ until they exchanged the glory of the immortal God for a worthless imitation, for the image of mortal man, of birds, of quadrupeds and ²⁴ reptiles. ·That is why God left them to their filthy enjoyments and the practices with which ²⁵ they dishonor their own bodies, ·since they have given up divine truth for a lie and have worshiped and served creatures instead of the creator, who is blessed for ever. Amen!

²⁶ That is why God has abandoned them to degrading passions: why their women have turned from natural intercourse to unnatural ²⁷ practices ·and why their menfolk have given up natural intercourse to be consumed with passion for each other, men doing shameless

things with men and getting an appropriate reward for their perversion.

²⁸ In other words, since they refused to see it was rational to acknowledge God, God has left them to their own irrational ideas and to ²⁹ their monstrous behavior. ·And so they are steeped in all sorts of depravity, rottenness, greed and malice, and addicted to envy, mur- ³⁰ der, wrangling, treachery and spite. ·Libelers, slanderers, enemies of God, rude, arrogant and boastful, enterprising in sin, rebellious to ³¹ parents, ·without brains, honor, love or pity. ³² They know what God's verdict is: that those who behave like this deserve to die—and yet they do it; and what is worse, encourage others to do the same.

☩

All people are unrighteous, all have sinned. Perhaps the pagans could argue that they have an excuse, since they do not have God's law to govern their lives. But Paul is quick to reject such an excuse (1:20-21). The wisdom tradition of the Old Testament concurred with that aspect of the Greek tradition which portrayed wise understanding as the ability to recognize the Creator in creation. The human spirit is capable of attaining wisdom to the extent that it can grasp the order of all created things (e.g., Ws 7:15-8:8, 13:1-9). Then the wise person is also holy and just because he or she recognizes and accepts the wisdom of the created world; but the sinner rejects creation's potential as a reflection of the glory of God (Rm 1:22-32). The created world revealed God so that all could know God (1:21). In modern theology, such reasoning as Paul uses has provided scriptural basis for the so-called natural law. In other words, the one who studies creation will be led to worship the Creator. The psalmist proclaimed the same message with the words: "To Yahweh belong earth and all it holds, the world and all who live in it" (Ps 24:1).

Those pagans who do not acknowledge God, who reject that the Creator can be found in creation, are culpable; they are under God's wrath (Rm 1:18). The anger of God is a metaphor describing God's just reaction to the pagans' sinfulness. Not to accept God's creation as a reflection of God is to deny one's own spirit, the spirit of wisdom (1:23-25). This is the height of stupidity which leads one into every kind of degradation and sin (1:26-32).

The pagans' vices, as Paul describes them, are base and degenerate (1:26-30). His list is probably borrowed from some Greek philosophers who denounced the outcasts in terms of lack of intelligence expressed in uncontrolled passions. Condemned were the ignorant, the mindless and unspiritual who led lives of licentiousness, sexual promiscuity, depravity. The basic sin lies in the rejection of wisdom —for Paul, God's wisdom. There are multiple expressions of this sin, but all have in common the characteristic Paul attributes to the pagans of substituting lower (i.e., according to the Greeks themselves, the more physical) for the higher (i.e., the spiritual) forms of life.

Stupidity gives honor to creatures rather than to the Creator. It is irrational and foolish to exchange the honor due the spiritual glory for the physical image (1:23). Paul is not against the body, nor does he exaggerate the significance of sexual sins (1:26–27). His argument is with those who degrade the body without being "wise" and thereby threaten human existence and its rightful dignity. The epitome of sanctity, achievable even for the pagans is a fully human life that witnesses to the right order of creation. The opposite is an impious and depraved life that refuses to honor or thank the Creator (1:18,21).

STUDY QUESTIONS: If God's everlasting power and deity are so plainly evident in creation, why is it so difficult for some of us to have faith in God and to obey his word? What are some signs of paganism you have witnessed even in Christians? Since it is so easy for some of us to go astray and not fully honor God as we should, does this mean that if we neglect God, he will abandon us forever? How is knowledge of God expressed in the honor paid to God?

Romans 2:1 – 3:20
THE TESTIMONY:
THE JEWS HAVE SINNED

Though not explicitly addressing them, Paul turns now to the Jews who were given the law and therefore had no excuse (2:1–3:20). The pagans have been convicted of sinning against their own consciences without the law (1:18–32). By their very act of judging others, those who have the law can see that their own sin is greater (2:1). Indeed, by their very judgment they invite the wrath of God because they cannot plead ignorance. God's patience is designed to bring all people to repentance (2:4). The fact that some have acquired sufficient knowledge to join in the judgment of God against the others who have sinned does not place the knowledgeable above sin, but only increases the responsibility to live according to what they *know* is true. But knowledge of what is right does not necessarily confer the power to act on this knowledge (cf. 7:18–23). Paul first shows that neither the law nor conscience provide exemptions from God's anger (2:1–29). But God's anger does not mean that God is unjust (3:1–8). Finally, Paul uses a composite of Old Testament quotations to show that the Scriptures themselves witness to the sin of all (3:4,10–20).

Romans 2:1–29
NEITHER THE LAW NOR CIRCUMCISION PROVIDES EXEMPTION FROM GOD'S ANGER

2 ¹ So no matter who you are, if you pass judgment you have no excuse. In judging others you condemn yourself, since you behave no ² differently from those you judge. ·We know that God condemns that sort of behavior impartially: ³ ·and when you judge those who behave like this while you are doing exactly the same, do you think you will escape God's ⁴ judgment? ·Or are you abusing his abundant goodness, patience and toleration, not realizing that this goodness of God is meant to lead you ⁵ to repentance? ·Your stubborn refusal to repent is only adding to the anger God will have toward you on that day of anger when his just ⁶ judgments will be made known. ·He will repay ⁷ each one as his works deserve. ·For those who sought renown and honor and immortality by always doing good there will be eternal life; ⁸ for the unsubmissive who refused to take truth for their guide and took depravity instead, ⁹ there will be anger and fury. ·Pain and suffering will come to every human being who employs himself in evil—Jews first, but Greeks ¹⁰ as well; ·renown, honor and peace will come to everyone who does good—Jews first, but ¹¹ Greeks as well. ·God has no favorites.

¹² Sinners who were not subject to the Law will perish all the same, without that Law;

sinners who were under the Law will have
¹³ that Law to judge them. ·It is not listening to
the Law but keeping it that will make people
¹⁴ holy in the sight of God. ·For instance, pagans
who never heard of the Law but are led by
reason to do what the Law commands, may
not actually "possess" the Law, but they can
¹⁵ be said to "be" the Law. ·They can point to
the substance of the Law engraved on their
hearts—they can call a witness, that is, their
own conscience—they have accusation and defense, that is, their own inner mental dialogue.
¹⁶ . . . on the day when, according to the Good
News I preach, God, through Jesus Christ,
judges the secrets of mankind.

¹⁷ If you call yourself a Jew, if you really trust
¹⁸ in the Law and are proud of your God, ·if
you know God's will through the Law and can
¹⁹ tell what is right, ·if you are convinced you
can guide the blind and be a beacon to those
²⁰ in the dark, ·if you can teach the ignorant and
instruct the unlearned because your Law em-
²¹ bodies all knowledge and truth, ·then why not
teach yourself as well as the others? You
²² preach against stealing, yet you steal; ·you
forbid adultery, yet you commit adultery; you
²³ despise idols, yet you rob their temples. ·By
boasting about the Law and then disobeying
²⁴ it, you bring God into contempt. ·As scripture
says: It is your fault that the name of God is
blasphemed among the pagans.

²⁵ It is a good thing to be circumcised if you
keep the Law; but if you break the Law, you
²⁶ might as well have stayed uncircumcised. ·If a
man who is not circumcised obeys the commandments of the Law, surely that makes up
²⁷ for not being circumcised? ·More than that,
the man who keeps the Law, even though he
has not been physically circumcised, is a living

condemnation of the way you disobey the Law
in spite of being circumcised and having it all
²⁸ written down. ·To be a Jew is not just to look
like a Jew, and circumcision is more than a
²⁹ physical operation. ·The real Jew is the one
who is inwardly a Jew, and the real circumcision is in the heart—something not of the letter
but of the spirit. A Jew like that may not be
praised by man, but he will be praised by God.

☩

The sinfulness of the pagans may be attested to by
their own consciences (2:15). The Jews, however,
have the law to accuse them. All, therefore, can be
guilty and thus stand under the anger of God. What
is revealed in the law has to be realized in the actions of people.

It is Paul who injected the concept of conscience
into the New Testament (2:15). Conscience has
even more importance in modern theological thinking than it had for Paul and certainly more than it
had for the other New Testament writers who practically ignored the concept (except Ac 23:1, 24:16;
Heb 9:9,14, 10:2,22, 13:18; 1 P 2:19, 3:16,21).
For Paul, conscience neither has the absolute, autonomous significance nor is it primarily interior as
its use usually suggests today. For Paul, conscience
here means the pagans' collective witness to what is
right (Rm 2:15). As use of the term in 1 Co
8:7,10–12 and 10:25–29 shows, conscience for Paul
is subject to the demands of mutual love, as members of one community in Christ. Paul's point in Rm

2:15 is that the pagans' conscience (i.e., their "inner mental dialogue") is in accord with the external witness of all the rest of creation.

As for the Jews, Paul continues, the fact that they live under the law does not place them above God's judgment (2:3–5). They must also obey the law. By the law, they profess to be teachers (2:17–24). But above all, they must practice the law they teach. Failure to do so convicts them while their own teaching accuses them (2:1).

Circumcision, as Paul goes on to say, is not only the initiation into Judaism (2:25–29); it seals and signs the covenant with God in man's flesh. Circumcision is the outward sign of willingness to serve God "with all your heart, with all your soul, with all your strength" (Dt 6:4). This sign is never conceived by Judaism as mere ritual; it is to be supplemented by an obedience to the whole law (Ga 5:3). Circumcision is like a promise to live one's whole life for God. If it is less than this, if it is an empty rite, it is a sign of condemnation. Circumcision must go deeper than the flesh, affecting the heart (Rm 2:29). It signifies a converted life.

Paul says a similar thing about the only appropriate context for celebrating the rite of the Lord's Supper in 1 Co 11:17–34. It must be in a setting where the community transcends normal social, economic, racial or political differences and divisions (e.g., 11:18,20). When disunity is allowed to overshadow the celebration, it is not the Lord's Supper that is commemorated; rather, it is Christians who eat and drink their own condemnation (1 Co 11:29). Symbols such as circumcision and the Eucharist, when divorced from the reality they represent, not only lose their meaning but become instruments of judgment against us.

STUDY QUESTIONS: Who should decide what good is? Is it ever legitimate to judge others? What kind of importance does Paul place on repentance? Does Paul teach that one pleases God only by doing good works?

Romans 3:1–8
YET GOD REMAINS FAITHFUL

¹ ² 3 Well then, is a Jew any better off? Is there any advantage in being circumcised? ·A great advantage in every way. First, the Jews are the people to whom God's message was ³ entrusted. ·What if some of them were unfaithful? Will their lack of fidelity cancel God's ⁴ fidelity? ·That would be absurd. God will always be true even though everyone proves to be false; so scripture says: In all you say your justice shows, and when you are judged ⁵ you win your case. ·But if our lack of holiness makes God demonstrate his integrity, how can we say God is unjust when—to use a human analogy—he gets angry with us in return? ⁶ That would be absurd, it would mean God ⁷ could never judge the world. ·You might as well say that since my untruthfulness makes God demonstrate his truthfulness and thus gives him glory, I should not be judged to be ⁸ a sinner at all. ·That would be the same as saying: Do evil as a means to good. Some slanderers have accused us of teaching this, but they are justly condemned.

✠

Since none are exempt from God's anger, we might be tempted to ask whether, then, there is any advantage to being a Jew, to having been entrusted with the law (3:2). Indeed, Paul answers, the law is a sign of the covenant; the will of God is revealed in the law. Today we might sometimes be tempted to put the question differently: if greater gifts carry greater responsibility, perhaps we would be better off without the gift. But this is an absurd denial of grace, a denial of personal identity, for what is a person without these gifts? The giving of the law to the Jews is what makes them the people of God. This is their identity. The law designates the Jews as the specially chosen people of God. Grace is God's free gift—acceptance of grace is the only response that is really human, for it is inhuman not to accept a life-giving gift and thereby recognize one's dependence on God. Even so, rejection or studied neglect of God's gift does not limit God or make God less generous. Even if all people, Jews and pagans alike, are completely unfaithful, God is not therefore less faithful (3:3-4). If human fidelity could force God to become less faithful or unfaithful, then humans would be gods, determining God. Humans would be capable of impoverishing God or of forcing God to react as they deserve rather than to act with integrity. But our lack of holiness only serves to demonstrate God's integrity (3:5).

Paul uses an anthropomorphism, that is, a human analogy, when he speaks of God's anger. The only just judge is God. The only just judgment appears to be the conviction of the world because of sin. In human terms, this seems like a manifestation of anger because it is a condemnation of the sin of the world. And yet a human analogy that makes God fit our image and likeness can lead to confusion, even absurdity (3:6-8). God's wrath is an expression of God's justice—yet God shows mercy in restraining anger and justifying the world.

STUDY QUESTIONS: What does Paul mean by the human analogy of the anger of God? Does Paul teach that circumcision is important to belief *and* holiness? If not, what is? On what basis does God make judgment? Does human infidelity provoke God's anger? Affect God's fidelity?

Romans 3:9–20
REVIEWING THE VERDICT:
ALL ARE GUILTY

⁹ Well: are we any better off? Not at all: as we said before, Jews and Greeks are all under ¹⁰ sin's dominion. ·As scripture says:

> There is not a good man left, no, not one:
> ¹¹ there is not one who understands,
> not one who looks for God.
> ¹² All have turned aside, tainted all alike;
> there is not one good man left, not a single one.
> ¹³ Their throats are yawning graves;
> their tongues are full of deceit.
> Vipers' venom is on their lips,
> ¹⁴ bitter curses fill their mouths.
> ¹⁵ Their feet are swift when blood is to be shed,
> ¹⁶ wherever they go there is havoc and ruin.
> ¹⁷ They know nothing of the way of peace,
> ¹⁸ there is no fear of God before their eyes.

¹⁹ Now all this that the Law says is said, as we know, for the benefit of those who are subject to the Law, but it is meant to silence everyone and to lay the whole world open to God's judg- ²⁰ ment; ·and this is because no one can be justified in the sight of God by keeping the Law: all that law does is to tell us what is sinful.

✠

The key for the whole of 1:18–3:31 is found in 3:9: "Jews and Greeks [i.e., pagans] are all under sin's dominion." Yet underlying this key verse is Paul's more basic assertion of faith that through the gospel all have access to the power of God for salvation (1:16–17). Paul proceeds from this assertion of faith to a demonstration that all must have had need for this power because all sinned. That is to say, all people lacked the power to save themselves. Paul moves here from the solution (i.e., salvation) to the plight of universal sinfulness. Paul had begun by arguing that the pagans are by definition sinners because they do not follow their own conscience and thus they bring upon themselves the anger of God (1:18).

Paul went on to say that the Jews' knowledge of the law (the very law that casts judgment on the pagans) does not exempt the Jews themselves from sin (2:1–29). The Jews are entrusted with God's law not because they are special, but they are special because they have been entrusted with the law of God (3:1–3). It is by God's mercy rather than because of their own sinlessness that the Jews are chosen and given the law. The law provides for violations against itself, but it also bears witness to the judgment that no one can be justified in the sight of God merely by keeping the law (3:20). A constant in the salvation history of Israel is the insistence on the sinfulness of the people. Particularly poignant is the infidelity of their leaders, who symbolize the complete unworthiness of all the people. The repeated message of the Old Testament is that God is faithful despite the faithlessness of the people. Time and again the people sin. Consistently God punishes them in order to bring them back. But God does not abandon them.

The Old Testament scriptures are replete with judgments issued against Israel's sinfulness. From Adam on, sin multiplies; no one is free from it. When he refers to "the Law," Paul includes not only the five books that comprise the Torah but all of the Hebrew scriptures. His most frequent references are to the Psalms and the prophets, especially Isaiah. For example, in 3:10–18, a collection of verses that testify to the fact that sin and degradation are universal, Paul's use of the Old Testament—Psalms and Isaiah—is typical of his style. What appears to us as eclectic, arbitrary selections to suit his own purpose is actually acceptable, legitimate practice, even for the Jews, in speaking to people who probably had no individual copies of the Old Testament for their own use, even were they able to read. It is probable that the early church used collections of Old Testament references called "testimonies" that listed frequently quoted passages. These testimony books would be especially practical for catechetical or missionary instruction and might also have been used to defend the church as it met with disbelief and downright opposition from those learned in the Old Testament. It seems that the testimonies arranged passages under certain themes for handy reference; such themes could have included universal sinfulness, the promise of God, the meaning of salvation.

STUDY QUESTIONS: No matter how good we try to be or how we try to live by the law, Paul says that every person is a sinner and unworthy. How then can a person hope to be acceptable to God? If the law does not really tell us what is good, but only what is sinful, how can we know what is good?

Romans 3:21-31
BACK TO SQUARE ONE:
GOD'S JUSTICE IS REVEALED

²¹ God's justice that was made known through the Law and the Prophets has now been re- ²² vealed outside the Law, ·since it is the same justice of God that comes through faith to everyone, Jew and pagan alike, who believes in ²³ Jesus Christ. ·Both Jew and pagan sinned and ²⁴ forfeited God's glory, ·and both are justified through the free gift of his grace by being re- ²⁵ deemed in Christ Jesus ·who was appointed by God to sacrifice his life so as to win reconciliation through faith. In this way God makes his justice known; first, for the past, when sins went unpunished because he held his hand, ²⁶ then, for the present age, by showing positively that he is just, and that he justifies everyone who believes in Jesus.

²⁷ So what becomes of our boasts? There is no room for them. What sort of law excludes them? The sort of law that tells us what to do? ²⁸ On the contrary, it is the law of faith, ·since, as we see it, a man is justified by faith and not ²⁹ by doing something the Law tells him to do. ·Is God the God of Jews alone and not of the pagans too? Of the pagans too, most certainly, ³⁰ since there is only one God, and he is the one who will justify the circumcised because of their faith and justify the uncircumcised ³¹ through their faith. ·Do we mean that faith makes the Law pointless? Not at all: we are giving the Law its true value.

✠

The justice of God is the power to save all. This power, given through the gospel of Christ, is accessible to all through faith (cf. 1:16–17). The law and the prophets initiated the revelation of God's justice (3:21). It was not God's revelation but the human vehicles that were inadequate both to transmit and to receive this justice. The law and its prophetic interpretations are essential stages in the progressive evolution of Israel's understanding of God. Both the law and its interpretation have run their course as effective means of revealing God's justice. Now faith has superseded boundaries set by the law and the prophets which differentiated the saved and the unsaved. The plight of both Jew and pagan was the same (3:23); Jesus became the redeemer, responsible for both (3:24).

God designated Jesus' life as sacred. Jesus sacrificed his life, winning reconciliation for all through faith (3:24–25). In 3:22–25, Paul refers to his thesis in 1:16–17—the gospel is the power of God for universal salvation. From this realization that all are saved through faith, Paul has argued that all Jews as well as pagans were in *need* of salvation (1:18–3:20). All needed time to grasp the message of salvation that included revelation of God's anger (1:18, 3:5). The period of the law and the prophets was characterized by sin—disobedience, rejection and divisions among people. All had the opportunity to recognize their own failure to achieve justice, which was the aim of both Old Testament piety and pagan reasoning.

God's justice, manifest in the justification of all who believe, is dynamic, powerful. Paul can almost be visualized searching for the images of sin and of grace he personifies later in this epistle (5:12–15). God's justice is more than merely present in the world; it acts. God's justice effects our justification (3:26). The dynamic reality which Paul describes also unifies those that the law separated (3:22–26). And this reconciliation occurs through the "free gift of [God's] grace." Justice, justification, redemption, faith, grace—these divine realities cannot be earned. It is imperative to note the consistent use of the passive voice in 3:21–26 where we are recipients and God is the initiator, the communicator, the giver of life. Justice "was made known [and] has now been revealed," both "Jew and pagan . . . are justified . . . by being redeemed." The "justice of God . . . comes . . . to everyone." "God makes his justice known," first, negatively and in the past, by holding back his hand and not punishing. Now, positively, by showing "that he is just and that he justifies everyone who believes in Jesus."

The Old Testament requires deeds and promotes division among people; the "law of faith" (3:27) excludes individual boasting. But faith and law are not usually associated by Paul as they are in 3:27. Here he uses the phrase "the law of faith" as the antithesis to the law which governs actions and considers human merit. Faith, on the contrary, is reliance on the fidelity of God who justifies "outside the Law" (3:21). God justifies not because we deserve justification but simply because the time of the revelation of God's justice has come. Further, Paul suggests that this justice and this faith effects horizontal as well as vertical reconciliation, that is, reconciliation with all people and, at the same time, reconciliation with God (3:24). Since we are redeemed by Christ, "by faith we are judged righteous and at peace with God" (5:1). And now, also through faith, Paul visualizes the reconciled state between "Jew and pagan alike" (3:22; cf. "everyone" in 3:22,26; "both" in 3:23,24). For the sake of opposing deeds and faith, Paul points to the positive aspects of the law, that is, not to what the law prohibits but to the fact that it dictates action and demands obedience. Thus, the law implies a merit system, making boasting possible, even probable (cf. 3:27). But the law of faith excludes boasting and joins all people in a common acknowledgment of one God.

The Jews themselves would recognize that there is only one God who is over pagans as well as Jews (3:29). The pagans' failure to recognize God did not detract from God's own identity. Whether all acknowledge God or not, the truth remains that there is but one God of all. And so it follows, as Paul suggests in 3:29–31, that faith is the link between God and people, and among all people. Faith justifies the circumcised and the uncircumcised (3:30). This realization does not affect the identity of the Jews as the people to whom the law is entrusted. Faith affirms the value and purpose of the law (3:31). The law is given in view of faith.

We have come full circle. Faith tells us we are all

ROMANS 3:21–31

saved through Jesus (3:21–26; cf. 1:16–17). Therefore, Paul reviewed the sin of all humanity that necessitated, indeed demanded, faith (1:18–3:20). The law made sin explicit, condemning both those under it and those outside it. Under the weight of its own condemnation, the law testified to the only hope for justification of everyone through faith.

STUDY QUESTIONS: What does Paul mean by saying that the "justice of God . . . comes through faith" (3:22)? With God's grace being a "free gift" to all who believe in Jesus, what obligation does one have for acceptance of such a free gift? Discuss what Paul means by "reconciliation through faith." Belief in Jesus sounds like the only prerequisite Paul teaches for our acceptance by God. This sounds simple. Is it? What is the difference between faith and doing what the law says to do? Is there any difference between the way the Jews and the way the pagans come to know God? What does Paul mean that faith gives the Law "its true value"?

Romans 4:1–8
THE WITNESS OF THE OLD TESTAMENT: ABRAHAM, OUR FATHER IN FAITH

¹ ² Apply this to Abraham, the ancestor from whom we are all descended. ·If Abraham was justified as a reward for doing something, he would really have had something to boast ³ about, though not in God's sight ·because scripture says: Abraham put his faith in God, and this faith was considered as justifying him. ⁴ If a man has work to show, his wages are not ⁵ considered as a favor but as his due; ·but when a man has nothing to show except faith in the one who justifies sinners, then his faith is con- ⁶ sidered as justifying him. ·And David says the same: a man is happy if God considers him righteous, irrespective of good deeds:

⁷ Happy those whose crimes are forgiven, whose sins are blotted out;
⁸ happy the man whom the Lord considers sinless.

✠

The ideas Paul has developed in 1:18–3:31 can be applied (as the Apostle demonstrates throughout Romans 4) to Abraham, the recognized father of Judaism (4:1). Abraham's greatness, all would readily agree, is his strong, courageous faith, rather than his works (4:3). And Abraham preceded the law.

He was justified "outside the Law" (3:21). It is typical of Paul to support his version of the gospel with examples from the Hebrew scriptures such as we find in his presentation of Abraham. He could not have found a more effective, popular figure to personify his teachings on justification by faith than Abraham.

The Jews would hardly need to review the story of Abraham (Gn 12:1–25:11) as we might. They would easily recall that Abraham was willing to leave his father's country in obedience to the call of God (12:1–3). Even more demanding, Abraham set out for the unknown, the land God promised to him. Faith motivated him to obey in pursuit of the promise. Faith overcame his fear of leaving the known for the unknown. God's call was given freely —Abraham had done nothing in particular to become worthy of its promise. So too the righteousness resulting from Abraham's faith was freely given. If the foundation is gift, the structure is gift also. Thus the idea of deeds and merit is futile. Paul offers as an analogy the model of a person who works for wages (Rm 4:4). Our economy-minded world can understand full well the implications of Paul's analogy, but we might find the mystery of the alternative (grace) hard to accept (4:5). An employer is not considered generous or beneficent or charitable when he pays the pre-agreed wages for a job. Conversely, an employer is unjust when he refuses to pay what is due.

The term "considers" (Rm 4:8) does not appear in Ps 32:1–2 which Paul is paraphrasing in Rm 4:7–8, but the gift idea is conveyed in our translation with "happy" to describe the state of the one whose sins are forgiven by God. Forgiveness is never really merited. God acts with the sinner who has faith in the same gracious way he treated Abraham, considering him or her justified. Faith is expressed as complete acceptance of God's forgiveness and God's justification. It is not that anyone is without sin. Rather, recognizing the sinfulness of all, believers accept the even greater, even more powerful consequences of justification.

STUDY QUESTIONS: Paul uses Abraham as an outstanding example of justification through faith. What did Abraham *do* to exhibit faith? If, in Romans 3, Paul says that all are sinful (cf. 3:9), what does he mean here by paraphrasing Ps 32:1–2 saying, "happy the man whom the Lord considers sinless" (4:8)?

Romans 4:9–12
ABRAHAM'S FAITH CAME
BEFORE CIRCUMCISION

⁹ Is this happiness meant only for the circumcised, or is it meant for others as well? Think of Abraham again: his faith, we say, ¹⁰ was considered as justifying him, ·but when was this done? When he was already circumcised or before he had been circumcised? It was before he had been circumcised, not after; ¹¹ and when he was circumcised later it was only as a sign and guarantee that the faith he had before his circumcision justified him. In this way Abraham became the ancestor of all uncircumcised believers, so that they too might ¹² be considered righteous; ·and ancestor, also, of those who though circumcised do not rely on that fact alone, but follow our ancestor Abraham along the path of faith he trod before he had been circumcised.

✠

In 4:9 Paul asks the Romans if the happiness Ps 32:1–2 refers to is only for those who are circumcised. The example of Abraham, he says, proves that it is not. Paul's point in choosing Abraham as the model of faith is to reinforce the gospel understanding that faith is greater than works. Abraham's faith was "considered"—that is, counted or reckoned in God's sight—as justifying him (Rm 4:3,9). The insistence on this term, which is used eleven times in Romans 4, underscores the gift aspect of justification as opposed to the notion of earning a wage or deserving justification because of works done.

Paul was probably aware of a tradition about Abraham he could have employed which emphasized his works, signified by his circumcision (Gn 17:9-14,23-27) and exemplified by his willingness to sacrifice Isaac (22:1-19). Such a tradition probably inspired Si 44:20-21 and Jm 2:21-22, for example, where accent is put on the fact that faith must be manifest in works. This seems to be the concern of James when he says, while appealing to the example of Abraham (2:21-23), "Faith without good works is useless" (2:20; cf. 2:24). But Paul neglects the concern of this tradition, using the same quotation as James does (2:23), to show rather the priority of Abraham's faith (Gn 15:6; Rm 4:3,9). Paul's rabbinic training might have served to support the priority of this text which comes before (i.e., in Genesis 15) the passages describing Abraham's obedient actions (i.e., in Genesis 17 and 22). The rabbis taught that whatever preceded in time took precedence over what follows. Along this line of reasoning, Paul argues that Abraham's faith in the promise is superior to his willingness to perform just deeds.

Since we are all descendants of Abraham, what was given to him affected not only Abraham himself but all those who are blessed in him according to the promise (Gn 12:1-3). Just as the sin of Adam (Rm 5:12-21) affected all who came after him, so the faith of Abraham affects all who hope to benefit from the promise entrusted to him. In other words, just as Abraham was justified because of his faith, so our faith justifies us.

STUDY QUESTIONS: What arguments does Paul use to show the difference between circumcision and faith, by appealing to the example of Abraham? How is circumcision a sign of faith?

Romans 4:13–17
FAITH IS THE PROMISE'S FOUNDATION

¹³ The promise of inheriting the world was not made to Abraham and his descendants on account of any law but on account of the ¹⁴ righteousness which consists in faith. ·If the world is only to be inherited by those who submit to the Law, then faith is pointless and the ¹⁵ promise worth nothing. ·Law involves the possibility of punishment for breaking the law—only where there is no law can that be avoided. ¹⁶ That is why what fulfills the promise depends on faith, so that it may be a free gift and be available to all of Abraham's descendants, not only those who belong to the Law but also those who belong to the faith of Abraham who ¹⁷ is the father of all of us. ·As scripture says: I have made you the ancestor of many nations—Abraham is our father in the eyes of God, in whom he put his faith, and who brings the dead to life and calls into being what does not exist.

☩

Jesus Christ fulfills the promise made to Abraham. Paul's whole perspective on reality is affected by the truth of Jesus Christ, revealed in the gospel. Through Jesus all have the free gift of faith. Because of the absolute nature of the free gift in Jesus, time loses significance. Abraham had access to this free gift before Jesus' time just as pagans and sinners now do (4:16). Previous revelations of God were partial; the fullness of revelation is now given, freely bestowed in Jesus.

Oftentimes it is helpful if we are able to identify a key verse that may unlock the full message of an entire passage. This is particularly true in Paul's writings where sometimes his thinking and method of development is foreign to ours and may appear strained or overdone. Such identification is a bit risky, too, since we may distort what Paul is saying by our own eagerness to make his reasoning fit what we determine is his main thought. Nevertheless, as long as we are willing to give Paul free rein and ride with an easy hold on some of his thoughts that could fall most naturally into his general gospel framework, the risk can be taken without fear of doing violence to the message. It seems legitimate for us to take such a risk here in Romans 4, in order to appreciate what Paul says about Abraham. Rm 4:16 provides a key that unlocks the meaning of the entire chapter. All Paul knows of God is revealed in "what fulfills the promise," that is, in Jesus.

STUDY QUESTIONS: How does keeping the law threaten to render faith pointless? Why does Paul say that the promise to Abraham depends on faith? Discuss the differences and relationship between faith and obedience.

Romans 4:18–25
ABRAHAM, MODEL OF FAITH

18 Though it seemed Abraham's hope could not be fulfilled, he hoped and he believed, and through doing so he did become the father of many nations exactly as he had been promised: Your descendants will be as many as the
19 stars. ·Even the thought that his body was past fatherhood—he was about a hundred years old —and Sarah too old to become a mother, did
20 not shake his belief. ·Since God had promised it, Abraham refused either to deny it or even to doubt it, but drew strength from faith and
21 gave glory to God, ·convinced that God had
22 power to do what he had promised. ·This is the faith that was "considered as justifying him."
23 Scripture however does not refer only to him but to us as well when it says that his faith was
24 thus "considered"; ·our faith too will be "considered" if we believe in him who raised Jesus
25 our Lord from the dead, ·Jesus who was put to death for our sins and raised to life to justify us.

✠

Abraham's was a hope against hope, a hope though all evidence was to the contrary. In his writings Paul seems to distinguish between faith (which is in God or in Jesus) and hope (whose object is God's promise). Even before the promise, Abraham believed. Later he believed even when the promise seemed unfulfillable (that is, when he considered his and Sarah's old age) and when it was threatened (that is, even when he was commanded to sacrifice Isaac) (4:18–20; Gn 17:1–2,15–22, 22:1–19). His faith was not dependent on what God did but on the God who did it. This is the kind of tenacious holding onto the God of surprises that is considered as justifying him (Rm 4:22). Despite all obstacles, in the face of clearly insurmountable human odds, Abraham believed and did not waver. He even grew strong in faith and that "gave glory to God" (4:20). Thus he is contrasted to the non-believers in 1:21 who did not give glory to God.

In the final verses of this chapter (4:23–25), Paul makes a distinct application of the meaning of Abraham's example for us. As 2 Tm 3:16 suggests, all scripture can be used for our instruction (cf. Rm 15:4). Paul, the pastor and first Christian writer, searched the scriptures not only to find ammunition to attack his opponents with or even to draw personal inspiration, but also to find responses to the challenge the scriptures pose for Christians. Faith still justifies as it justified Abraham. Our faith will be considered our justification by the same God whom Abraham believed in and who raised Jesus from the dead.

The conclusions of some of the sermons of Acts (e.g., Ac 2:23–24, 3:15–16, 4:10) seem to emphasize the polemic aspect of Jesus' death at the hands of "sinful men" (Lk 24:7). The scriptures, especially Isaiah 53, aid Paul to see the positive redemptive nature of Jesus' death for our sins. Jesus' being raised from the dead is the central element of faith which nevertheless rests on the historical fact of his death. Faith makes it possible for "sin" and "death" to not be the last words and for Jesus not to be merely a criminal condemned to death two thousand years ago but our risen Lord. Faith enables us to be like Abraham, to hold on to the impossible even when we consider our own inadequate bodies (Rm 4:19). Faith enables us to see past our own sin and its consequence in death to the God of the Resurrection.

Paul says that if Jesus has not been raised, then our faith is in vain (1 Co 15:14–17). The early Christians, like Paul, shared the conviction that the Good News conveyed by the Resurrection is that death is not the last word and that all the human sin, expressed in the betrayal, denial and failure not only of Jesus' enemies but also of the Apostles and disciples, could not destroy the life given by God in Jesus. The gospel of salvation was written in the light of the Resurrection experience. The gospel reveals that Jesus conquered sin and death and restored all people to life. The basic gospel conviction, then, is one of faith in the Resurrection. Whereas the death of Jesus was historically verifiable, the Resurrection is a faith conclusion. This faith interprets the scandal of Jesus' death as redemptive, for our sins. And because God raised Jesus from the dead (cf. 1 Co 15:15; 2 Co 4:14; Ga 1:1 and passim), he has been given the name "Lord," by which Christians recognize him (cf. Rm 10:9).

STUDY QUESTIONS: Paul sets up Abraham as the prime example of faith, yet Abraham did not know Jesus. Why then should we try to know Jesus? Did Jesus, like Abraham, have faith? Is it possible for doubt to coexist with faith?

Romans 5:1 – 8:39
NEW LIFE IN CHRIST

Rm 5:1–8:39 continues Paul's description of the tensions experienced by the Christians who have been liberated from sin (1:18–3:31, 5:12–21), death (6:1–23) and the law (7:1–25) and who believe that they have been given righteousness and now are at peace with God (5:1–11, 8:1–39). Despite the sufferings they still must endure, they live with hope, which they know is well grounded in God's own action through Christ (cf. 5:3–5, 8:18–39).

In 5:1–11, Paul returns to the thesis he articulated in 1:16–17 that the power which is the source of Christian hope is in the gospel of Jesus Christ, not dependent on human merit. In 6:1–8:39 the implications of the contrast Paul set up in 5:12–21, with his description of the first and the second Adam, are clarified. If it is a foregone conclusion—a generally accepted fact—that the sin of Adam had universal, wide-ranging repercussions, how much more comprehensible, Paul argues, is the conviction that the second Adam, Christ, had a deeper and more powerful sphere of influence. So Christ has done for us what we could not do for ourselves. It may seem as if sin demanded and received the gracious reaction of God that salvation is. If this is true, one may suggest, it would be better to sin more so that more grace will be given. Paul already anticipated this objection in 3:5-8. Now, he almost appears to resign himself to the need to deal with it in case anyone following him could possibly have missed so much of what he has said that they could stubbornly continue to object. With an emphatic disclaimer, Paul answers his own rhetorical question (6:1): "Should we remain in sin so as to let grace have greater scope?"

Paul, even with his strong conviction about the new life in Christ, had to admit that sin and the law are formidable foes. Implicit in the rhetorical question are more subtle ones—apparently less blatantly obtuse, but nevertheless threatening because they seem valid: What if sin still holds its sway? What if our experience of sin is so formidable as to discourage faith in grace? In plain terms, if grace is so powerful to effect its own ends, why do we need to be so concerned about fighting sin? Sin is still very much with us—that is one angle of the problem that faces even the most sincere listener of Paul. What the Apostle could seem to be saying is that we can relax —grace will prevail. Misunderstood, Paul seems to be giving license to sin.

Some interpreters seem to oversimplify Paul's notion of salvation as described in 5:1-11 and 8:1-39. They tend to emphasize the dichotomy between works and faith, reducing salvation to a once-and-for-all conversion experience which renders the verdict that works are meaningless. Romans 6 and 7 represent Paul's description of a more developmental process of conversion. Chapter 6 speaks of the power of sin as if to warn against complacency, which might lull one back into slavery to unrighteousness. Chapter 7 shows the power of the law which produces awareness of the impossibility of saving ourselves. In 5:12–7:25, Paul deals with the universality of sin and sin's chaotic effects manifested in death (6:1–23) and the function of the law (7:1–25). Paul's reflections on the universal nature of sin (5:12–7:25) is enveloped in the Apostle's consideration of the powerful, universal effects of justification through Christ (cf. 5:1–11 and 8:1–39).

The overall form of Paul's thesis and its development in Romans is based on that of the philosophical diatribe. This form is characterized by significant rhetorical questions that indicate the progressive stages of the argument (e.g., 3:1–9, 6:1,15, 7:7, 9:6,14, 10:18, 11:1). That is to say, Paul proceeds in Romans by presenting a vehement, argumentative discourse to dissenting interlocutors (real or imaginary) whose objections Paul anticipates with judiciously placed rhetorical questions. Key verses throughout the epistle state these questions and serve as indicators of the progress of Paul's argument. Paul raised some crucial questions in 3:1–9 which he attempts to answer in the course of this epistle. He presents his arguments in dialogue with would-be interlocutors who challenge his positions and explanations. A question he takes up in Romans 6 is one implied in 3:7–8: If untruthfulness makes God demonstrate his glory, why are we judged sinners? In Romans 6 and 7 the diatribe tone and style is intensified. Romans 6 responds to the retort that if sin makes grace abound, as Paul maintains in 5:18–21, then "we should remain in sin so as to let grace have greater scope" (6:1). But this is absurd. Romans 7 goes on to show that living under the law when we have already died to the law is equally meaningless. The style of the dialogue will reappear in Romans 9–11 after Paul develops his description of Christian life in chapter 8, an integral part of the unit with 5:1–7:25.

Romans 5:1–11
BY FAITH WE ARE
AT PEACE WITH GOD

5 ¹ So far then we have seen that, through our Lord Jesus Christ, by faith we are judged ² righteous and at peace with God, ·since it is by faith and through Jesus that we have entered this state of grace in which we can boast ³ about looking forward to God's glory. ·But that is not all we can boast about; we can boast about our sufferings. These sufferings bring pa- ⁴ tience, as we know, ·and patience brings per- ⁵ severance, and perseverance brings hope, ·and this hope is not deceptive, because the love of God has been poured into our hearts by the ⁶ Holy Spirit which has been given us. ·We were still helpless when at his appointed moment ⁷ Christ died for sinful men. ·It is not easy to die even for a good man—though of course for someone really worthy, a man might be pre- ⁸ pared to die—·but what proves that God loves us is that Christ died for us while we were still ⁹ sinners. ·Having died to make us righteous, is it likely that he would now fail to save us from ¹⁰ God's anger? ·When we were reconciled to God by the death of his Son, we were still enemies; now that we have been reconciled, surely we may count on being saved by the life ¹¹ of his Son? ·Not merely because we have been reconciled but because we are filled with joyful trust in God, through our Lord Jesus Christ, through whom we have already gained our reconciliation.

✠

At this point, 5:1–11 appears like an oasis of promise and hope between the descriptions of universal sin (1:18–3:20 and 5:12–21) and sin's chaotic effect (6:1–7:25). Together with Romans 8, 5:1–11 is surely one of the most inspirational and hope-filled passages of the New Testament. Paul, the original Christian writer, is thinking through the great Christian message. The realities affected by this message are the basis of his unshakable hope in even greater blessing to come; we are justified, we are judged righteous, we are at peace, we have been reconciled, God's love has been abundantly poured into our hearts (5:1,5,10–11). It is essential to note that the verbs, in the perfect tense, describe the present reality of already being "right" with God. It is God who has set us right through Jesus (5:6–10). God's gift to us in Jesus is a reconciliation that goes beyond the chaos caused by our sin. If becoming righteous were up to us, the picture would be dismally discouraging. But it is not. God's grace, more powerful by far than human sin, has set us right and enabled us to live in peace with God and with one another (5:10–11).

The effects of the peace Jesus has won for us cannot be overestimated. Peace for Paul is so much more than an absence of conflict or a patching up of quarrels. God's own peace is shared with us. This is the integrity of God as described in the lesson of Mt 5:43–48: God does not act or react on the basis of human merit but lets the rain and sun be for the honest and the dishonest alike (5:45). This is peace such as Paul describes it in Ph 4:4-9: the more we ponder God's own peace, the more it will reign in our hearts to banish all ignoble, unvirtuous, unjust thoughts. The experience of God's peace abundantly bestowed on us is blessing itself and a foretaste of participating in ever greater glory (Rm 5:1,5,11).

Often boasting represents the fundamentally sinful attitude for Paul, for it has its roots in pride. Self-sufficiency inflates the ego (cf. 1 Co 8:1) and its boastful expression is the opposite of love (cf. 13:4). But boasting is not merely unattractive, it is sinful. Boasting refers back to self as the source of confidence, and when that confidence is rooted in fearful competition, it divides. It stifles community. Grace is the outpouring of love into our hearts (Rm 5:5). Grace is the gift of the spirit that empowers us to create community. But the spirit of God enables us to overcome personal self-centeredness. The source of the Christians' confidence is not self but the reconciliation given to them by Jesus. The basis for Christian boasting is a surprise to the world: it is the cross. Christians boast of their suffering (5:3). They do not live in the world without tension; they experience conflict with the values of the world. Such conflict schools the believer in Christian values, especially in persevering hope (5:4). The very positive tone of Paul's thoughts does not qualify in the least the promise of suffering that awaits the committed Christian (cf. 5:3, 8:18).

There is a strong, persistent *now* emphasis in this passage. We are already judged righteous, we are *now* at peace (5:1). Now we suffer; now we test patience. We have hope because we are reconciled. Hope is often portrayed as relating to the future; but its strength lies in being able to live in the now. Hope is experienced as a positive reflection on the possibilities of living in conflict. Hope allows us to affirm the promise of God amid the conflicts and tensions of everyday life. It is not likely that since Christ has already died for us to make us righteous, God will abandon us now. Thus we have firm reason to expect God's glory (5:2).

STUDY QUESTIONS: How are Jesus and faith related here in Romans 5? What is meant by a "state of grace" (5:2)? How does the Holy Spirit bring about salvation? According to 5:9–10, we have been reconciled and can count on being saved. Is there any difference between salvation and reconciliation? Why?

Romans 5:12–21
THE FIRST AND THE SECOND ADAM

¹² Well then, sin entered the world through one man, and through sin death, and thus death has spread through the whole human ¹³ race because everyone has sinned. ·Sin existed in the world long before the Law was given. There was no law and so no one could be ac- ¹⁴ cused of the sin of "lawbreaking," ·yet death reigned over all from Adam to Moses, even though their sin, unlike that of Adam, was not a matter of breaking a law.

¹⁵ Adam prefigured the One to come, ·but the gift itself considerably outweighed the fall. If it is certain that through one man's fall so many died, it is even more certain that divine grace, coming through the one man, Jesus Christ, came to so many as an abundant free ¹⁶ gift. ·The results of the gift also outweigh the results of one man's sin: for after one single fall came judgment with a verdict of condemnation, now after many falls comes grace with ¹⁷ its verdict of acquittal. ·If it is certain that death reigned over everyone as the consequence of one man's fall, it is even more certain that one man, Jesus Christ, will cause everyone to reign in life who receives the free gift that he does not deserve, of being made ¹⁸ righteous. ·Again, as one man's fall brought condemnation on everyone, so the good act of one man brings everyone life and makes them ¹⁹ justified. ·As by one man's disobedience many were made sinners, so by one man's obedience ²⁰ many will be made righteous. ·When law came,

it was to multiply the opportunities of falling, but however great the number of sins committed, grace was even greater; •and so, just ²¹ as sin reigned wherever there was death, so grace will reign to bring eternal life thanks to the righteousness that comes through Jesus Christ our Lord.

☩

Using the Adam story in 5:12–21, Paul recapitulates the universal implications of sin that he argued in 1:18–3:20. The story of Adam can be called a "myth" in the sense that it is a symbolic representation of theological truths in story form. These truths lie in the universal nature of sin that has affected human experience since the beginning of time, that is, since the first person was created and soon thereafter sinned. With the story of Adam the biblical writers tried to balance their belief in the absolute goodness of God who could not have created evil, with their awareness that since the beginning, humankind has experienced the consequences of sin. Death, for example, is a consequence of sin that has been felt since Adam. Genesis (1:26–27, 2:7–25) tells the story of creation; in 3:1–24, immediately following these creation accounts, we find the record of the first sin, punishment and the veiled prediction of redemption in terms of the conflict between the offspring of the serpent (i.e., evil) and the offspring of the woman (i.e., humankind) which will result in her descendants crushing the head of the evil one (cf. 3:15). The story of Adam, then, conveys the near originality of sin, i.e., the conviction that although God created only "good" (1:31), the pall of death, sin's consequence, was over all humanity almost from its creation (3:19; cf. Rm 5:12).

As in 1:18–3:31, Paul stresses faith in a reality more powerful and far-reaching than the human dilemma of sin. The general, universal end of human life is death. This is clear from all experience. But as fundamental as this observation is, Christian faith is even more basic as an alternative given by God through grace (5:17). Death appears to conquer, make void all that life means. But the free gift of grace in Jesus brings life that is eternal. Sin abounds but grace abounds more (5:20). Even if sin exercises power over life, the life in Christ who was raised from the dead is even more powerful (5:21).

Paul's method of proceeding is by *a fortiori* argumentation, a method generally accepted by the rabbis. It is abundantly clear that death is universal and that death is the consequence of the human work of sin (5:12). Therefore it is all the more clear that the free gift of grace has power that far exceeds the limited but universal consequence of human sin (5:19–21).

STUDY QUESTIONS: Did God intend for us to sin? How does the comparison between Adam and Christ demonstrate the more powerful effects of grace? Did God plan sin in order to offer his free gift of Jesus to the undeserving? Do we have freedom to accept or reject this gift?

Romans 6:1–14
THE LIBERATION OF BAPTISM

¹ ² Does it follow that we should remain in sin so as to let grace have greater scope? ·Of course not. We are dead to sin, so how can we ³ continue to live in it? ·You have been taught that when we were baptized in Christ Jesus we ⁴ were baptized in his death; ·in other words, when we were baptized we went into the tomb with him and joined him in death, so that as Christ was raised from the dead by the Father's glory, we too might live a new life.

⁵ If in union with Christ we have imitated his death, we shall also imitate him in his resurrec- ⁶ tion. ·We must realize that our former selves have been crucified with him to destroy this sinful body and to free us from the slavery of ⁷ sin. ·When a man dies, of course, he has finished with sin.

⁸ But we believe that having died with Christ ⁹ we shall return to life with him: ·Christ, as we know, having been raised from the dead will never die again. Death has no power over ¹⁰ him any more. ·When he died, he died, once for all, to sin, so his life now is life with God; ¹¹ and in that way, you too must consider yourselves to be dead to sin but alive for God in Christ Jesus.

¹² That is why you must not let sin reign in your mortal bodies or command your obedi- ¹³ ence to bodily passions, ·why you must not let any part of your body turn into an unholy weapon fighting on the side of sin; you should, instead, offer yourselves to God, and consider

yourselves dead men brought back to life; you should make every part of your body into a
¹⁴ weapon fighting on the side of God; ·and then sin will no longer dominate your life, since you are living by grace and not by law.

☩

If, as Paul insisted in Romans 5, God's gift of grace to us outweighs our sin, it may seem to follow that we should remain in a sinful state so as to benefit more fully from the more powerful gift of grace. Now, in 6:1-14, Paul resorts to a temporal argument. We have already died to sin through Baptism; we cannot rescind the better condition. We cannot return to the weaker condition of our former life if we have truly died. Addressing Christians who are already baptized (cf. 6:4), Paul uses the fact that the saving effects of Baptism have already begun. Baptism puts us in a *state* of reconciliation that completely removes us from our former state of sin. The person who would protest that according to Paul's own argument more sin only means more grace does not grasp how radical and irreversible is the transformation of grace.

The term "baptism" itself means immersion. This was literally signified in ancient ritual but is more symbolic in most Christian rites of Baptism today. Paul's concern is clearly not with the rite itself or the formulas used in Baptism, but with the reality Baptism represents of immersion into Christ. This immersion into Christ's death and Resurrection is as irrevocable as the saving event itself. It is unthinkable to cross back over into the realm of death once one has been baptized into life with Christ.

Paul's Baptism theology is the basis of his mystical union-with-Christ description of Christian life. Fully immersed into Christ, we have died with him and are alive with him (6:8). Our sinful inclinations were just as truly crucified and killed as Christ was (6:5–11). And now we are fully alive to God through the Resurrection. Just as Christ is.

Baptism is the symbol of Christian inclusiveness that became for Paul the focus of the gospel preaching. Baptism effectively eliminates any distinction between the saved and the unsaved because Baptism is accessible to all through faith. Faith, for Paul, is commitment to Christ. That is, through faith we are associated with and made one with Christ, in his death and Resurrection. Paul has described death as the consequence of sin. Now he shows Christ's death to be a consequence of his obedience, his submission to God expressed in the fullness of Christ's humanity (Ph 2:7–8). The justification Christ won for us is union with him in his death and Resurrection. These become real for us in Baptism.

Although Baptism is, for Paul, the symbol of Christian life, he rarely develops his teaching on Baptism itself. Romans 6 is therefore an exception. In fact, in 1 Co 1:14–17, Paul expresses grateful relief that he has baptized so few people because the Corinthians were using the baptismal minister as a rallying point to cause divisions in the community. Thus, Paul seems to have little interest in Baptism as a rite, yet he gives great significance to the effects of Baptism as symbolizing union with Christ.

The Jews were baptized into Moses (1 Co 10:2) and lived out this baptism by obedience to the law. Christians are baptized into Christ (Rm 6:3). They have been crucified *with* Christ so as to be risen *with* Christ. Death and life are two opposite, mutually exclusive states. Since we are either dead or alive, the choice of which power we serve has to be complete.

STUDY QUESTIONS: Is our being under grace rather than sin a simple matter of a decision of the will or an intellectual choice? What does commitment to God mean? If we are not free to sin, are we free?

Romans 6:15-23
THE CHOICE:
SLAVERY TO SIN OR TO GOD

15 Does the fact that we are living by grace and not by law mean that we are free to sin?
16 Of course not. ·You know that if you agree to serve and obey a master you become his slaves. You cannot be slaves of sin that leads to death and at the same time slaves of obedience that
17 leads to righteousness. ·You were once slaves of sin, but thank God you submitted without
18 reservation to the creed you were taught. ·You may have been freed from the slavery of sin, but only to become "slaves" of righteousness.
19 If I may use human terms to help your natural weakness: as once you put your bodies at the service of vice and immorality, so now you must put them at the service of righteousness for your sanctification.
20 When you were slaves of sin, you felt no
21 obligation to righteousness, ·and what did you get from this? Nothing but experiences that now make you blush, since that sort of behav-
22 ior ends in death. ·Now, however, you have been set free from sin, you have been made slaves of God, and you get a reward leading to your sanctification and ending in eternal life.
23 For the wage paid by sin is death; the present given by God is eternal life in Christ Jesus our Lord.

✠

Paul picks up in 6:15–23 one of his favorite images, that of slavery, to describe the difference between the former life of sin and life in the service of righteousness (6:18). Paul contrasts sin and righteousness as two opposing powers, two masters. Paul's view of the human condition necessitated postulating that we serve some spiritual power, either good or evil. This perspective helps Paul describe the problem of the incomplete status of our Christian freedom while we are yet in the process of recognizing the total demands of our allegiance to Christ who is Lord. It is clear for Paul that we are not masters of our own lives. The direction of our lives is determined by the power of either good or evil that rules us. As Jesus said, "No one can be the slave to two masters" (Mt 6:24). He implies that we are the slave of one. The forces that control human lives are *kyrioi,* lords, masters. Commitment is made either to good or to evil, to the reign of God or to demonic forces. Our slavery is to one or the other. Paul seems to be less concerned with individual, concrete actions than with the life of service for good or for evil that is the product of our choice.

The life of grace excludes the slavery to sin. It is not typical of Paul to link freedom and sin as he does in the rhetorical question in Rm 6:15. This connection betrays the confusion of his supposed opponents. Having formerly been slaves to sin, the baptized are now obedient to righteousness. The title to ownership has been transferred. The Christian has been given over to the creed he or she has been taught (6:17). Here Paul presents the Christian creed as a kind of master, a phrase which is unusual for him (6:16). Although faith is a kind of submission (the Greek roots of "faith" and "obedience" are related), Paul does not usually reduce faith to creed. Yet the idea of slavery either to evil, represented by sin which is personified and presented as a kind of master who "entered" the world with the first Adam, or to God is typical of Paul. By speaking of the Christian's submission to a creed, Paul might have wished to remove any misunderstanding of Baptism or faith conceived as merely an initial rite without practical implications. Christian life means integrity between belief and practice, faith and service.

For Paul, then, slavery is not really a negative concept. Paul describes his own apostolic call and mission as slavery to Jesus Christ (1:1; Ga 1:10; cf. 1 Co 7:22). This is a service freely given. It liberates from the slavish subjection to law, sin and death. Slavery to God inserts one into the world of the second Adam where grace abounds.

By Rm 6:19, nevertheless, Paul himself seems to be aware of the limitations of his contrast between two types of slavery. The conditions are too radically different to be expressed by the same image of slavery. The real meaning is deeper, existentially rooted. The contrast would be better expressed in the difference between slavery and freedom which appears in 8:21, for example. The former life of sin was characterized by shame, the frustration of being reduced to slavishness despite good intentions, reaping only the earnings of guilt (6:21,23). These are all part of the experience of being overpowered, seduced, dominated and diminished by evil. But the Christian has been brought to life and light in Christ. Through faith we are free to serve righteousness (6:18). Instead of being obsessed by shame and guilt, the person of faith can serve God in righteousness. Paul opposes the wages of sin to the unexpected, undeserved *rewards* of righteousness (6:23). This righteousness is not to be postponed until "eternal life," but begins in this world as we learn to give ourselves progressively to the service of the gospel (6:19). Serving God in righteousness means the promotion of God's kingdom of justice already here. The righteousness of God empowers believers as a very concrete, real power to be used in this world to oppose the powers of sin which enslave.

Almost as if to anticipate one last objection of his imaginary interlocutor, Paul postpones developing the meaning of freedom until Romans 8. In Romans 7 he turns his attention to a final protest that still dogs the would-be convert—that is, what about the role of the law?

STUDY QUESTIONS: How comfortable would you be if all your thoughts and actions were open to scrutiny? Could they be imitated by those who depend on you for guidance? Does Paul mean we should seek God in order to be rewarded? In 6:15-23, Paul presents God and Jesus in terms of a gift, and the offer of a gift requires a recipient and response. How does our response evidence itself?

Romans 7:1-6
FREED FROM THE CONTRACT WITH DEATH

¹ Brothers, those of you who have studied law will know that laws affect a person ² only during his lifetime. ·A married woman, for instance, has legal obligations to her husband while he is alive, but all these obligations ³ come to an end if the husband dies. ·So if she gives herself to another man while her husband is still alive, she is legally an adulteress; but after her husband is dead her legal obligations come to an end, and she can marry someone else without becoming an adulteress. ⁴ That is why you, my brothers, who through the body of Christ are now dead to the Law, can now give yourselves to another husband, to him who rose from the dead to make us ⁵ productive for God. ·Before our conversion our sinful passions, quite unsubdued by the Law, fertilized our bodies to make them give ⁶ birth to death. ·But now we are rid of the Law, freed by death from our imprisonment, free to serve in the new spiritual way and not the old way of a written law.

✠

We come now to Romans 7, one of the most controversial and often quoted passages in Paul's letters and perhaps in all of the New Testament. With this passage it suddenly seems to become less significant to debate whether Paul is addressing the Jews specifically when he calls his readers "brothers . . . who have studied the law" (7:1; cf. 2:17) or whether he means to include a more general audience. What he says about the law in Romans 7 could refer to the Torah or it could refer to any legal ordinance. Nor does it really matter that his analogy of the married woman freed from her husband after his death (7:2–3) collapses when we try to apply it too rigidly. What Paul means has general implications. He shows that the law is powerless to give life; although it defines good and evil, it can do nothing to bring about good (7:7–23). Thus we depend on God to do what the law was unable to do (cf. 8:3, 7:24–25).

Paul's message in Romans 7 is not confined to a consideration of the role of the law in the early church, as seems to be the case in Romans 9–11 (cf. esp. 9:4, 10:4–8). In Romans 7 Paul's point is more basic and universal. Paul shows how the law fulfilled its role in defining what is evil (7:7–11). Yet while the law also brought the knowledge of what is right, it could not enable anyone to do what is right (7:15–23). And so the law contributed to the hopelessness of our condition before Christ (7:24). The law made clear our need for grace.

Paul begins his description of the role of the law by stating the obvious: the living, not the dead, are bound by the law (7:1). He uses a human analogy. A woman is bound by the law to her husband while he is living, but the bond is broken when he dies (7:2–3). The analogy cannot be forced. His point is clear in 7:4: so "you [as Christians] can now give yourselves to another husband, to him who rose from the dead to make us productive for God." This conclusion is based on the discussion of Romans 6 where Paul showed that the Christian, through Baptism, died to sin (6:4–11). The analogy limps because the husband is supposed to represent the law, but the Christian is freed not by the law's death but by his or her own death through Baptism. But the lesson of the analogy is that the Christian is no longer dominated by the law with its characteristics of sin and death.

The phrase "before our conversion" (7:5) means, literally, "while we were in the flesh." The "flesh" can mean the material side of our nature (cf. 1 Co 15:39) or even the whole of our earthly existence, as in 2 Co 10:3. For Paul it most often refers to the pre-Christian propensity for sin. The law could not subdue or control our passions which produced our death (Rm 7:5). But through the body of Christ, we died to the law and became productive for God (7:4). The former, unconverted way was one of death, imprisonment by the law and uncontrolled passions; now rid of the law, we are free to serve in the spiritual way (7:6).

STUDY QUESTIONS: Is the law necessary? Why? Discuss the dichotomy Paul makes between imprisonment in the law and spiritual freedom.

Romans 7:7–25
THE LAW CONTRIBUTES THE KNOWLEDGE OF SIN

⁷ Does it follow that the Law itself is sin? Of course not. What I mean is that I should not have known what sin was except for the Law. I should not for instance have known what it means to covet if the Law had not ⁸ said You shall not covet. ·But it was this commandment that sin took advantage of to produce all kinds of covetousness in me, for when there is no Law, sin is dead.

⁹ Once, when there was no Law, I was alive; but when the commandment came, sin came ¹⁰ to life ·and I died: the commandment was meant to lead me to life but it turned out to ¹¹ mean death for me, ·because sin took advantage of the commandment to mislead me, and so sin, through that commandment, killed me.

¹² The Law is sacred, and what it commands ¹³ is sacred, just and good. ·Does that mean that something good killed me? Of course not. But sin, to show itself in its true colors, used that good thing to kill me; and thus sin, thanks to the commandment, was able to exercise all its sinful power.

¹⁴ The Law, of course, as we all know, is spiritual; but I am unspiritual; I have been sold as ¹⁵ a slave to sin. ·I cannot understand my own behavior. I fail to carry out the things I want to do, and I find myself doing the very things ¹⁶ I hate. ·When I act against my own will, that

means I have a self that acknowledges that
¹⁷ the Law is good, ·and so the thing behaving in that way is not my self but sin living in me.
¹⁸ The fact is, I know of nothing good living in me—living, that is, in my unspiritual self—for though the will to do what is good is in me, the
¹⁹ performance is not, ·with the result that instead of doing the good things I want to do, I carry out the sinful things I do not want.
²⁰ When I act against my will, then, it is not my true self doing it, but sin which lives in me.
²¹   In fact, this seems to be the rule, that every single time I want to do good it is something
²² evil that comes to hand. ·In my inmost self I
²³ dearly love God's Law, but ·I can see that my body follows a different law that battles against the law which my reason dictates. This is what makes me a prisoner of that law of sin which lives inside my body.
²⁴   What a wretched man I am! Who will rescue
²⁵ me from this body doomed to death? ·Thanks be to God through Jesus Christ our Lord!
  In short, it is I who with my reason serve the Law of God, and no less I who serve in my unspiritual self the law of sin.

✠

Paul's discussion of the law entangles him in several thorny issues which necessitate his returning to the defense of the law's positive function (7:7–25; cf. 3:31 and Ga 3:21–22). It is as if the Apostle has so interwoven the characteristics of the law and sin that he anticipates his readers' confusion of the two. Some might even think, from what Paul says, that sin and the law are identical (Rm 7:7). Paul's review of the law's record has not been very positive (3:20, 4:15, 5:20, 7:4–6; Ga 3:10–11,19–20). He can avoid the question no longer (Rm 7:7): "Does it follow that the Law itself is sin?" At last, in 7:7–25 he takes the time to consider his negative answer to this question. The way 7:7–13 is seen influences our understanding of Paul's answer.

Focusing on the observation that Paul speaks in the first person singular (7:7–25), many interpreters understand this text as mainly autobiographical. Others emphasize Paul's use of the past tense in 7:7–13 as contrasted with the present tense in 7:14–25. This contrast describes the futile struggle within oneself before conversion as opposed to life after conversion. A combination of these two proposed interpretations probably renders the best understanding of 7:7–25. Paul reflects on his own experience as representative of the collective experience of anyone before conversion. His use of "I" is a rhetorical device expressing the profoundly personal yet generally relevant experience of all people.

There are strong merits of this interpretation. If 7:7–25 were merely autobiographical, this description would contradict the self-assured portrait of Paul's life under the law (cf. Ga 1:13–14; Ph 3:4–6), which he described as "faultless" (Ph 3:6). If Rm 7:7–25 describes primarily the internal conflict of an individual racked with guilt, such a description seems to betray obsessive characteristics not typical of Paul. Generally, the Apostle shows more interest in the communal, relational transformations effected by conversion to Christ. Rm

ROMANS 7:7–25

7:7–25 represents Paul's third attempt in this epistle to demonstrate the plight of all people (himself included) because of the universal effects of sin. In 1:18–3:20 he showed these effects by demonstrating that both divisions of humankind, pagans and Jews alike, have sinned. In 5:12–21 he pointed out that the sin of the first man, Adam, was passed on to all people since Adam. Now, in probably the most powerful description of all, he shows the universality of sin by describing the wretched (7:24) condition of all until rescued in Jesus Christ (7:25).

The poignancy of the human dilemma of powerlessness in sin, despite the law, is expressed in the tortured exclamation and question of 7:24: "What a wretched man I am! Who will rescue me from this body doomed to death?" The situation under the law seems to be hopeless. But it is not. Our hope is grounded not in the law but in Jesus, the rescuer. God does what the law could not do (8:3). Paul returns to the original positive note of 1:16–17. Thus he begins and ends this doctrinal section (1:18–8:39) with a description of the saving power of God (8:1–39).

STUDY QUESTIONS: Does the law do anything more than label our activities as sin? How does Paul define the function of the law? Does Paul suggest there is benefit and good within sin? How can the law be both practicable and spiritual? Can we ever hope to be free from sin and truly spiritual? If so, when? And how?

Romans 8:1-13
FREEDOM IN THE SPIRIT

¹⁻² 8 The reason, therefore, why those who are in Christ Jesus are not condemned, ·is that the law of the spirit of life in Christ Jesus has set you free from the law of sin and death. ³ God has done what the Law, because of our unspiritual nature, was unable to do. God dealt with sin by sending his own Son in a body as physical as any sinful body, and in that body God condemned sin. ⁴ ·He did this in order that the Law's just demands might be satisfied in us, who behave not as our unspiritual nature but as the spirit dictates.

⁵ The unspiritual are interested only in what is unspiritual, but the spiritual are interested in spiritual things. ⁶ ·It is death to limit oncself to what is unspiritual; life and peace can only come with concern for the spiritual. ⁷ ·That is because to limit oneself to what is unspiritual is to be at enmity with God: such a limitation never could and never does submit to God's law. ⁸ ·People who are interested only in unspiritual things can never be pleasing to God. ⁹ Your interests, however, are not in the unspiritual, but in the spiritual, since the Spirit of God has made his home in you. In fact, unless you possessed the Spirit of Christ you would ¹⁰ not belong to him. ·Though your body may be dead it is because of sin, but if Christ is in you then your spirit is life itself because you ¹¹ have been justified; ·and if the Spirit of him who raised Jesus from the dead is living in

you, then he who raised Jesus from the dead will give life to your own mortal bodies through his Spirit living in you.

12 So then, my brothers, there is no necessity for us to obey our unspiritual selves or to live
13 unspiritual lives. ·If you do live in that way, you are doomed to die; but if by the Spirit you put an end to the misdeeds of the body you will live.

☨

Romans 8 is less like a conclusion to the preceding than a restatement and development of the implications of Paul's original thesis in 1:16–17. In 8:1–39 Paul reveals the foundation of his undauntable hope, not so much in spite of the wretchedness of the human condition he has described (cf. 1:18–3:20; 5:12–7:25), but because his more basic conviction is in the power of God to give justification to all (cf. 1:16–17, 3:21–5:11). Paul's gospel insight is rooted in God who makes salvation accessible to all through grace. Thus, Paul is inspired to say, "What we suffer in this life can never be compared to the glory as yet unrevealed" (8:18). Paul's discussion in Romans 8 hinges on the tension between the spiritual and the unspiritual (8:1–13) and our adoption by the Spirit as the children of God (8:14–30). Paul concludes this chapter with a hymn celebrating God's love (8:31–39).

The opposition between the spiritual and the unspiritual (8:1–13) is not created by Paul but rather adapted from the Greeks. For them, the antithesis was between spiritual ideals, which were the only realities, and material reflections, which were mere shadows of the real. The Greeks expressed this tension as experienced in the human condition in terms of the tug of war between the "spirit" (i.e., the mind, soul, life principle, temperament—the reality that animates our flesh) and the "body" (i.e., the material, flesh, corporeal parts of a human being). For Paul, both the spirit and the body, when subjected to the "law of the spirit of life in Christ Jesus" are "free from the law of sin and death" (8:2–3) as he described them in 6:1–7:25. Those "who are in Christ Jesus" (8:1) are rescued from death (7:24), which seemed like the only hopeless fate until the Spirit came (8:13). But now the "love of God has been poured into our hearts by the Holy Spirit" (5:5). The Spirit governs the actions of those who are in Christ, enabling them to overcome the limits of the unspiritual and to concern themselves with life and peace (8:5–7; cf. Ga 5:16–26).

STUDY QUESTIONS: What is the "law of the spirit"? What is Christian freedom? How is it different from license? What does Paul mean by "unspiritual"? Is freedom a dangerous idea?

Romans 8:14-30
THE SPIRIT REVEALS THE CHILDREN OF GOD

¹⁴ Everyone moved by the Spirit is a son of
¹⁵ God. ·The spirit you received is not the spirit of slaves bringing fear into your lives again; it is the spirit of sons, and it makes us cry out,
¹⁶ "Abba, Father!" ·The Spirit himself and our spirit bear united witness that we are children
¹⁷ of God. ·And if we are children we are heirs as well: heirs of God and coheirs with Christ, sharing his sufferings so as to share his glory.
¹⁸ I think that what we suffer in this life can never be compared to the glory, as yet unre-
¹⁹ vealed, which is waiting for us. ·The whole creation is eagerly waiting for God to reveal
²⁰ his sons. ·It was not for any fault on the part of creation that it was made unable to attain its purpose, it was made so by God; but crea-
²¹ tion still retains the hope ·of being freed, like us, from its slavery to decadence, to enjoy the same freedom and glory as the children of
²² God. ·From the beginning till now the entire creation, as we know, has been groaning in
²³ one great act of giving birth; ·and not only creation, but all of us who possess the first-fruits of the Spirit, we too groan inwardly as
²⁴ we wait for our bodies to be set free. ·For we must be content to hope that we shall be saved —our salvation is not in sight, we should not
²⁵ have to be hoping for it if it were—·but, as I say, we must hope to be saved since we are not

saved yet—it is something we must wait for with patience.

26 The Spirit too comes to help us in our weakness. For when we cannot choose words in order to pray properly, the Spirit himself expresses our plea in a way that could never be
27 put into words, ·and God who knows everything in our hearts knows perfectly well what he means, and that the pleas of the saints expressed by the Spirit are according to the mind of God.

28 We know that by turning everything to their good God co-operates with all those who love him, with all those that he has called according
29 to his purpose. ·They are the ones he chose specially long ago and intended to become true images of his Son, so that his Son might be
30 the eldest of many brothers. ·He called those he intended for this; those he called he justified, and with those he justified he shared his glory.

✠

Paul intensifies his description of life in the Spirit in 8:14–30. Everyone moved by the Spirit of God has a new identity as children of God. Formerly slaves of sin, we are now animated by God's spirit which makes us heirs. The diametrical opposition between the condition of slaves and that of heirs was already developed in Ga 3:23–4:31. There Paul was attempting to describe the temporary and insufficient role of the law now superseded by Christ. Having described the hopelessness of the human condition before faith in Rm 6:1–7:25, Paul in 8:14–30 merely refers to the former "spirit of slaves" (8:15), but more fully develops the contrasting characteristics of God's children. It is the Spirit which enables us to identify God as "Abba, Father" (8:15; Ga 4:16). By the Spirit we become heirs as God's children, coheirs with Christ (Rm 8:17) who became the eldest of many (8:29). Christ's Resurrection was like a promise to us of what we will become, for by his Resurrection, Christ became the "first-fruits" (1 Co 15:23; cf. Col 1:15,18). We are intended to be the true images of Christ (Rm 8:29; 1 Co 15:49; Ph 3:21). The Spirit is "the pledge of our inheritance" (Ep 1:13-14). He passes to us the "first-fruits of the Spirit" as we wait for our bodies to be set free (Rm 8:23).

Freedom is not entirely ours yet. We are no longer slaves who live in the spirit of fear (8:15), but we are waiting with all of creation for the full revelation of the children of God (8:19-25). The fact of suffering implies that the fullness of this revelation is yet to come. The enslavement of all creation itself (8:20-21), as well as our own sharing in the sufferings of Christ (8:17), represents the labor pains that must be endured in order to give birth to God's children (8:22-23). And regardless of how acute the suffering we witness is, it cannot be compared, Paul says, to the glory that is to come (8:18). The Apostle himself gives eloquent testimony to his faith in the infinite richness of God's mercy, which surpasses all understanding, in Romans 9-11 when he takes up the personally excruciatingly painful question of Israel's rejection of the gospel. This causes a sense of religious pain tempting the believer to despair. But Paul commits his own experience and the suffering of the Jews temporarily excluded from the gospel to the mercy of God who "has imprisoned all . . . in their own disobedience only to show mercy to all" (11:32). Israel represents one example of how "creation . . . was made unable to attain its purpose . . . by God" (8:20), not through its own fault but as part of God's plan (8:28–30, 11:25–36).

STUDY QUESTIONS: How can a person know he or she is "moved by the Spirit" (8:14)? Discuss the child/"Abba" relationship Paul refers to here. What is the redeeming aspect of human suffering, according to Paul? Do you think Paul's description is overly optimistic? What is the Spirit that Paul speaks of and how can the Spirit help us? To be "called according to [God's] purpose" (8:28) could sound selective, but could Paul himself mean this since he envisions salvation as universal? How can one know he or she has been called?

Romans 8:31–39
WHEN GOD ACQUITS, COULD ANYONE CONDEMN?

³¹ After saying this, what can we add? With
³² God on our side who can be against us? ·Since God did not spare his own Son, but gave him up to benefit us all, we may be certain, after such a gift, that he will not refuse anything he
³³ can give. ·Could anyone accuse those that God
³⁴ has chosen? When God acquits, ·could anyone condemn? Could Christ Jesus? No! He not only died for us—he rose from the dead, and there at God's right hand he stands and pleads for us.

³⁵ Nothing therefore can come between us and the love of Christ, even if we are troubled or worried, or being persecuted, or lacking food or clothes, or being threatened or even at-
³⁶ tacked. ·As scripture promised: For your sake we are being massacred daily and reckoned as
³⁷ sheep for the slaughter. ·These are the trials through which we triumph, by the power of him who loved us.

³⁸ For I am certain of this: neither death nor life, no angel, no prince, nothing that exists,
³⁹ nothing still to come, not any power, ·or height or depth, nor any created thing, can ever come between us and the love of God made visible in Christ Jesus our Lord.

✠

When Paul was able to express his faith that God, cooperating with all who love him, converts everything to their good (8:28), he feels he has nothing more to add (8:31-39). He has consistently pointed out that part of the struggle of our human condition is due to the fact that we are necessarily dominated by some spiritual force, for good or for evil, which is stronger than we are. But this struggle is reduced to insignificance when we realize that God struggles on our side. Again Paul returns to his initial thesis: the gospel is the power of justification for all who believe (1:16-17). In other words, nothing "can ever come between us and the love of God made visible in Christ Jesus our Lord" (8:39). The ultimate gift of God's love was his son (8:32; cf. 5:6-11; Jn 3:16). God did not send his son to condemn us but to justify us (Rm 8:1-4,34). When this verdict of God's love is spoken, sin's sentence of death cannot hurt us. So firm is the believing Paul's faith in this that all else that could possibly threaten us is reduced to nothing in the light of this reality (8:38-39). Paul's indomitable hope rests in the power of the love of God, not in any created thing. Equipped with such hope, Paul is enabled to consider the potentially devastating problem of Israel's rejection of the gospel of Christ in Romans 9-11. It is as if, in naming the possible threats to the gospel as revelation of Christ's love, Paul is forced to remember the fact that it is his very faith in the gospel which separates him from his own people. It is as if his hope, which knows no bounds (cf. 15:13) must yet be submitted to the bitter test of the experience of his own people.

And Paul's own experience reveals the true strength that comes from suffering in the example of Christ. As Paul testifies in 2 Co 4:8-10:

> We are in difficulties on all sides, but never cornered; we see no answer to our problems, but never despair; we have been persecuted, but never deserted; knocked down, but never killed; always, wherever we may be, we carry with us in our body the death of Jesus, so that the life of Jesus, too, may always be seen in our body.

STUDY QUESTIONS: What can threaten to separate us from the love of God? What threatens to separate us from the love of one another? Are some separations and divisions all right?

Romans 9:1 – 11:36
THE PLACE OF ISRAEL IN GOD'S PLAN FOR UNIVERSAL SALVATION

Romans 9–11 appears in stark contrast to the hymn that closed Romans 8 and summed up Paul's theology in the first doctrinal part of this epistle. Immediately following the outburst of hope that characterized chapter 8, the reader is not prepared for the return of the diatribe style (see the introduction to Rm 5:1–8:39, pp. 172–75) so intensified in tone, that marks the progress of Paul's development in Romans 9–11 (cf. 9:6,14, 10:18–19, 11:1,11). These three chapters are set off from their context, Romans 8 and 12, by a distinct introduction (9:1–5) and conclusion (11:33–36). This has prompted some interpreters to suggest that Paul inserted a previously independent treatise on the perplexing problem of Israel's rejection of the gospel, which represented Paul's best efforts to reconcile this rejection with God's fidelity as it was being revealed in history. While it would be an exaggeration to separate completely Romans 9–11 from the doctrinal development of Romans 1–8, it is possible to treat Romans 9–11 as a relatively discrete or independent unit with its own unique properties.

Although he identified himself as the Apostle to the pagans, Paul could not dismiss the problems raised by Israel's failure as a whole people to accept the gospel he preached. Paul was a Jew, steeped in Jewish tradition and theology. But the questions he struggles with regarding Israel are not merely personal ones, nor is his preoccupation limited to the way his own people are reacting to his preaching. Paul tries to articulate a theodicy, that is, a vision of God which must necessarily incorporate the characteristics, such as fidelity and justice, which Israel has always recognized as divine. Paul concentrates in Romans 9–11 on the problem of God rather than on the problem of Israel. He wrestles with the very possibility of faith in a God such as the Old Testament describes. And Paul does not sound like an objective bystander, least of all in this discussion which involves his own God and his own people. In Romans 9–11 we see the Apostle engaged in a struggle to defend the very identity and credibility of God. This issue of God's fidelity is the primary point of Paul's wrestling with the question of Israel's rejection of the gospel. The Apostle understands this not as a merely human, provisional or temporary problem but as one that affects the very foundation of a Christian understanding of God because it brings the fidelity of God into question.

To put it another way, the church now composed of both pagans and Jews, was laying claim to the promises originally entrusted to Israel. Paul identifies this church as the "Israel of God" (Ga 6:16). Such claims seem to betray a grave injustice. Further, they seem to be a very shaky basis on which to build Christian theology. Paul's reflections raise several questions he himself seems to be struggling with. Why, for example, should God be more faithful to the church than to the chosen people, the Jews, whom he seems now to reject? Is the time of the Jews over? Did God put a limit on it despite the promises to the contrary? How can Paul preach that God's promises have been extended to the pagans when they have not even been fulfilled among the Jews? All of these questions tormented Paul (and undoubtedly the early church as well), and Romans 9–11 presents dramatic evidence that Paul suffers intensely to find how Israel fits into the plan of a faithful God.

Romans 9–11, dealing with the place of Israel in salvation history, is appropriately inserted in a letter Paul writes to a mixed community, where Jewish Christians seem to have been in the minority and may even have been oppressed (cf. Introduction to Romans, pp. 117–23, above). Generally, Paul seems to be inclined to defend the pagans' place in the church (e.g., Ga 2:1–21). Now, perhaps, he feels obligated to defend the Jews' place in the church and at the same time, to defend himself against the accusation of being a traitor to his own people. He incorporates this defense as an integral part of his gospel which must not be misconstrued as being anti-Jewish just because he is so pro-pagan. It is clear from reading Romans 9–11 that Paul's heart is bound to his own people (e.g., Rm 9:1–5, 10:1–2, 11:1–2). Nowhere in the epistle does the Apostle seem more passionately involved. He seeks to resolve this problem because it brings into question the very fidelity of the God which he preaches as Apostle to the pagans and it also brings into question the salvation of the Jews who reject Christ. In a sense, Paul does not come up with any solution at all except to reaffirm his faith in both God and Israel. He demonstrates that, although all Israel is not Israel (9:6), some have been saved. And so, he proclaims, "the rest of Israel will be saved as well" (11:26).

In Romans 9–11, then, "Israel" is a theological rather than merely a historical or ethnic concept. Israel represents the people of God of whom some are yet being identified. Paul does not at all exclude the Jews from salvation. The temporary rejection of the gospel by some Jews has a positive purpose for the final acceptance by all (11:11–32). In this passage, then, Israel represents the promise of universal salvation. The result of this promise, part of the mystery of God and being worked out in human history (11:25–36), is that eventually all Israel, that is, all people, will be saved.

Romans 9:1–5
"THE PROMISES WERE MADE TO THEM"

9 ¹ What I want to say now is no pretense; I say it in union with Christ—it is the truth—my conscience in union with the Holy Spirit ² assures me of it too. ·What I want to say is this: my sorrow is so great, my mental anguish ³ so endless, ·I would willingly be condemned and be cut off from Christ if it could help my brothers of Israel, my own flesh and blood. ⁴ They were adopted as sons, they were given the glory and the covenants; the Law and the ritual were drawn up for them, and the prom- ⁵ ises were made to them. ·They are descended from the patriarchs and from their flesh and blood came Christ who is above all, God for ever blessed! Amen.

✠

The contrast between 9:1–5 and the preceding verses, 8:31–39, is striking. After reading Paul's magnificent profession of faith that nothing "can come between us and the love of Christ" (8:35), it is startling to have the Apostle swear such love for his own people that, he says, he would even be willing to be cut off from Christ (9:3) if that could help Israel. So strong is Paul's love and concern for the

Jews that he counters his own indomitable optimism with consideration, in Romans 9–11, of probably one of the greatest, most painful questions facing the early church, namely, the Jews' rejection of the gospel. More correctly, Paul's focus is on the problem this poses for faith in God's justice and fidelity; in other words, he asks, how is God faithful in the light of the present rejection of the gospel by the Jews which seems to exclude them from the new Israel?

This three-chapter reflection on the fidelity of God in view of the gospel's unacceptability to the Jews refers back to questions Paul already raised but did not develop in 3:1–9. More specifically, Paul posed the question very explicitly which could not but torment him greatly, in 3:3–4:

> What if some of them [i.e., the Jews] were unfaithful? Will their lack of fidelity cancel God's fidelity? That would be absurd. God will always be true even though everyone proves to be false. . . .

Only the utterly loveless could fail to appreciate the experience of agony Paul expresses in 9:1–5. The Apostle is torn apart by his love for and loyalty to his own people as he realizes that they are rejecting the gospel he is committed to preaching to the pagans. The remainder of this chapter (9:6–33) surveys the past, reviewing God's predilection for Israel as recorded in the Old Testament. With many examples, Paul will drive home the awareness that God acts in freedom to name his chosen people, independently of the expectations of human systems (e.g., the more powerful, the eldest, the more loyal, etc.). In this introductory statement of 9:1–5, Paul capsulizes the history of Israel's privileges. Here he also testifies to his love for his Jewish kin, to whom he is joined by bonds of blood, theological convictions, common history (esp. 9:1–3).

Paul intones his review of Israel's privileges with a dramatic avowal of his own fidelity to the Jews and an appeal to the witness of his own conscience to the truth of this love (9:1–2). He even expresses his willingness to be cut off from Christ, who for Paul gives meaning to his life (cf. Ga 2:20) *if that would be of any service to his own people* (Rm 9:3). But it would not. The Jews are themselves separated from Christ—by their rejection of the gospel. This is true even though they are people whose very history is punctuated by innumerable gifts from God—covenants, the law, the promises, the patriarchal models, even the Christ (9:4–5).

STUDY QUESTIONS: Why does Paul feel such deep anguish about Israel? Whom does Paul refer to when he speaks of "my brothers of Israel"? Why do you think he must defend his love for his own people?

Romans 9:6–33
NOT ALL DESCENDANTS FROM ISRAEL ARE ISRAEL

6 Does this mean that God has failed to keep his promise? Of course not. Not all those who 7 descend from Israel are Israel; ·not all the descendants of Abraham are his true children. Remember: It is through Isaac that your name 8 will be carried on, ·which means that it is not physical descent that decided who are the children of God; it is only the children of the promise who will count as the true descend- 9 ants. ·The actual words in which the promise was made were: I shall visit you at such and 10 such a time, and Sarah will have a son. ·Even more to the point is what was said to Rebecca when she was pregnant by our ancestor Isaac, 11 but before her twin children were born and before either had done good or evil. In order 12 to stress that God's choice is free, ·since it depends on the one who calls, not on human merit, Rebecca was told: the elder shall serve 13 the younger, ·or as scripture says elsewhere: I showed my love for Jacob and my hatred for Esau.

14 Does it follow that God is unjust? Of course 15 not. ·Take what God said to Moses: I have mercy on whom I will, and I show pity to 16 whom I please. ·In other words, the only thing that counts is not what human beings want 17 or try to do, but the mercy of God. ·For in scripture he says to Pharaoh: It was for this I raised you up, to use you as a means of

showing my power and to make my name
known throughout the world. ·In other words, when God wants to show mercy he does, and when he wants to harden someone's heart he does so.

You will ask me, "In that case, how can God ever blame anyone, since no one can oppose his will?" ·But what right have you, a human being, to cross-examine God? The pot has no right to say to the potter: Why did you make me this shape? ·Surely a potter can do what he likes with the clay? It is surely for him to decide whether he will use a particular lump of clay to make a special pot or an ordinary one?

Or else imagine that although God is ready to show his anger and display his power, yet he patiently puts up with the people who make him angry, however much they deserve to be destroyed. ·He puts up with them for the sake of those other people, to whom he wants to be merciful, to whom he wants to reveal the richness of his glory, people he had prepared for this glory long ago. ·Well, we are those people; whether we were Jews or pagans we are the ones he has called.

That is exactly what God says in Hosea: I shall say to a people that was not mine, "You are my people," and to a nation I never loved, "I love you." ·Instead of being told, "You are no people of mine," they will now be called the sons of the living God. ·Referring to Israel Isaiah had this to say: Though Israel should have as many descendants as there are grains of sand on the seashore, only a remnant will be saved, ·for without hesitation or delay the Lord will execute his sentence on the earth. As Isaiah foretold: Had the Lord of hosts not

left us some descendants we should now be
like Sodom, we should be like Gomorrah.

³⁰ From this it follows that the pagans who were not looking for righteousness found it all the same, a righteousness that comes of ³¹ faith, ·while Israel, looking for a righteousness derived from law failed to do what that law ³² required. ·Why did they fail? Because they relied on good deeds instead of trusting in faith. In other words, they stumbled over the ³³ stumbling stone ·mentioned in scripture: See how I lay in Zion a stone to stumble over, a rock to trip men up—only those who believe in him will have no cause for shame.

✠

In 9:6–33, Paul surveys Israel's past, searching for a response to two related questions. The first concerns God's fidelity to his promise (9:6) and the second is about God's justice (9:14). In 9:6–13, Paul takes up the first question, showing the fidelity of God by using a series of Old Testament examples of how the principle of selectivity was used to insure the preservation of God's chosen people. Paul's examples would appeal to his Jewish hearers. A quick check of the Old Testament history rendered well-known illustrations of how God's fidelity was manifested in choices that defied human preconceptions of justice and made clear the truth that "not all those who descend from Israel are Israel" (9:6). Paul ticks off his examples, illustrating his enormous command of the Old Testament literature. Abraham's name was carried on through Isaac even though he was younger than Ishmael, Abraham's son through the slave woman (9:7). This was a result of the promise of God (cf. 9:8-9; cf. Ga 4:21-31). God's choice of Jacob over Esau was totally free (Rm 9:10-13), manifest "before either had done good or evil" (9:11). So God worked among the patriarchs, freely choosing whomever he wanted to and considering whomever he wanted to as bearers of his promise. These examples are at the heart of Israel's self-identification and show God's fidelity to his people.

God's choice also distinguished Israel from her enemies, protecting Israel and insuring the promise which began with Abraham and was renewed through such examples as Paul uses (i.e., Isaac, Jacob).

In 9:14-33, Paul turns to his second question which could seem to some to be inevitably problematic because of what he has said so far, "Does it follow that God is unjust [9:14]?" It might seem that since God does choose whomever he wants, God's justice is questionable. Paul responds with an unqualified "No" and then proceeds to recall some examples which, again, his Jewish audience in particular would probably find acceptable. It is clear that God's choice of Israel over the Pharaoh (9:14-17) was based in God's own merciful choice of Israel rather than on human merit. And this is not only an example of ancient history showing how God worked at the time of Moses. Paul broadens the parameters of his response, quoting the prophets Isaiah and Hosea so that everyone can see the justice of God's free preference to choose whomever he will, either to "show mercy" or to "harden someone's heart" (9:18). We are like clay in the hands of a potter, unable to protest the shape into which we are molded (9:20-21). God spoke in a similar way through Hosea and his word alone transformed a non-people into the children of "the living God" (9:25-26).

In fact, Paul alternates between a lesson of history which many in his audience could easily accept and a demonstration of the free action of God which continues to choose people in the present. Paul admits no dichotomy between God's freedom, fidelity, justice and mercy. They are all interrelated as various expressions of God's grace being revealed in history. Previously, for example, God's freedom insured his fidelity to Abraham although not through all his descendants. Also previously, God's justice showed mercy to Israel and hardened the hearts of Israel's enemies (e.g., Egypt). The prophets continually reminded the Israelites that they were distinguished from the pagans not because they were better, but because they had been chosen to become God's own. Constantly, too, Israel was reminded that all were not faithful and that only a remnant would be saved (9:27). By implication Paul anticipates what he will say in 11:5: "Today the same thing has happened: there is a remnant, chosen by grace." Paul's purpose is not only to explain the place of Israel as a nation, but to stress the reality of grace in the life of every person.

STUDY QUESTIONS: What experiences of God's mercy can you identify in your own life? What did Paul have in mind when he reviewed Israel's experience of mercy? How can Paul equate justice and mercy? Do you think that justice means that God treats everyone equally? Is God's plan as the Old Testament presents it as clear as Paul tries to make it? How can a person fully trust in faith?

Romans 10:1-21
THE WORD IS NEAR

¹ ² ³ Brothers, I have the very warmest love for the Jews, and I pray to God for them to be saved. ·I can swear to their fervor for God, but their zeal is misguided. ·Failing to recognize the righteousness that comes from God, they try to promote their own idea of it, instead of submitting to the righteousness of ⁴ God. ·But now the Law has come to an end with Christ, and everyone who has faith may be justified.

⁵ When Moses refers to being justified by the Law, he writes: those who keep the Law will ⁶ draw life from it. ·But the righteousness that comes from faith says this: Do not tell yourself you have to bring Christ down—as in the ⁷ text: Who will go up to heaven? ·or that you have to bring Christ back from the dead—as in the text: Who will go down to the under- ⁸ world? ·On the positive side it says: The word, that is the faith we proclaim, is very near to ⁹ you, it is on your lips and in your heart. ·If your lips confess that Jesus is Lord and if you believe in your heart that God raised him from ¹⁰ the dead, then you will be saved. ·By believing from the heart you are made righteous; by confessing with your lips you are saved. ¹¹ When scripture says: those who believe in him ¹² will have no cause for shame, ·it makes no distinction between Jew and Greek: all belong to the same Lord who is rich enough, however

¹³ many ask his help, ·for everyone who calls on the name of the Lord will be saved.

¹⁴ But they will not ask his help unless they believe in him, and they will not believe in him unless they have heard of him, and they will not hear of him unless they get a preacher,
¹⁵ and they will never have a preacher unless one is sent, but as scripture says: The footsteps of those who bring good news is a welcome
¹⁶ sound. ·Not everyone, of course, listens to the Good News. As Isaiah says: Lord, how many
¹⁷ believed what we proclaimed? ·So faith comes from what is preached, and what is preached comes from the word of Christ.

¹⁸ Let me put the question: is it possible that they did not hear? Indeed they did; in the words of the psalm, their voice has gone out through all the earth, and their message to the
¹⁹ ends of the world. ·A second question: is it possible that Israel did not understand? Moses answered this long ago: I will make you jealous of people who are not even a nation; I will make you angry with an irreligious people.
²⁰ Isaiah said more clearly: I have been found by those who did not seek me, and have revealed myself to those who did not consult me;
²¹ and referring to Israel he goes on: Each day I stretched out my hand to a disobedient and rebellious people.

☩

Having reviewed how God's grace has affected Israel's past (9:6–33), Paul turns now in 10:1–21 to a description of the present. He begins by repeating his devotion to his own kinspeople and testifies to their zeal for God (10:1–3). Yet this very zeal prevents them from recognizing the truth of the gospel Paul preaches. The gospel reveals that "now the Law has come to an end with Christ, and everyone who has faith may be justified" (10:4). By submitting to a death which was cursed by the law (cf. Dt 21:23; Ga 3:13–14), and by his Resurrection, Christ superseded the limits of the law. That is to say, whereas through the law Christ was put to death, God raised him from the dead, and by the Resurrection overturned the verdict of the law. Through the Resurrection, Christ became the Lord of all (Rm 10:9). Christ's becoming the Lord brought an end to any "distinction between Jew and Greek" (10:13) which the law had dictated. Now justification comes to any who "call on the name of the Lord" (10:13).

Paul addresses his brother Christians (10:1), protesting his love for his kinspeople, the Jews. By their common faith, Paul and all Christians have become "family" to one another, bonded to one another by ties that supersede former familial, blood or ethnic relationships. It is partly Paul's consciousness of this new, deeper bond with Christians that prompts his defense of his loyal concern for the Jews. The Apostle opened Romans 9 and will begin Romans 11 with a comparable testimony to the turmoil of his apostolic yet Jewish heart (cf. 9:1–5, 11:1–2). Rooted in Judaism, he *feels* uprooted and estranged from his own people. In anguished rather than accusing tones, he identifies their misguided zeal as the source of their blindness. His former experience as a persecutor of the church because of zeal for the law (Ga 1:13–14; Ph 3:4–6) undoubtedly tempered his indignation, prevented any trace of self-righteousness and dictated his compassionate understanding, his non-judgmental testimony of the Jews' integrity.

Paul is agonized about the present situation of his own people who do not accept the end of the law (Rm 10:4). Typically, he looks for inspiration in the Old Testament and finds that the present situation is consistent with the past. The law and the prophets whom he quotes in 10:5–21 showed the remarkable fidelity of God even when the people were obstinate and rebellious. Paul really does not yet draw any conclusions about Israel when he assesses the present in 10:1–21. But he might have discovered one source of consolation in the realization that what he witnesses is not new. Israel's former obstinacy did not alter the fidelity of God, so perhaps her present rejection of the gospel will not make God less faithful either.

In 10:5–13 there is a strong tension between the law and faith. The law is described as written by Moses (10:5), who is usually a negative figure in Paul's epistles. In contrast, the righteousness of faith speaks as if it were a living voice (10:6). Then Paul goes on to describe this righteousness, by borrowing from Deuteronomy, a book of the law. His selective use of the Old Testament undoubtedly appears less arbitrary when we realize that he might have used an existing Jewish Midrash, i.e., a running commentary on an Old Testament passage used for teaching purposes. The text from Deuteronomy describes the law as being within Israel's reach (10:8). Paul applies the basic idea of this text to Christ, adapting the images of ascent into heaven and descent into the underworld to Christ's life, death and Resurrection. Christ has brought the Word "that is the faith we proclaim" near (10:8). The Word is accessible to all. Paul's emphasis on the elements of faith (believe in your heart) and confession (confess with your lips) reflects the fact that faith is not a purely individual or interior matter. Faith has a dimension of mutual encouragement and challenge so that members of the Christian community acknowledge publicly that Jesus is Lord. Confession of the Lordship of Jesus, who is over all, is an outward expression of faith. Faith means that the law, which distinguishes the Jew from the Greek (cf. 10:12), came to an end (10:4). Confession unifies members of the one community, for Christ, as Ep 2:14–15 says, has "broken down the barrier which used to keep them apart, actually destroying in his own person the hostility caused by the rules and decrees of the Law."

Finally, in Rm 10:5–13, Paul identifies a fundamental relationship between Christ's Resurrection and his Lordship over all. Jesus died, submitting to the curse of the law (Ga 3:13–14). Such was his obedience to God. Because of this obedience, God raised him from the dead, thereby going beyond the law. Now Christ, not the law, is Lord of all who believe. And all have access to Christ by faith, since the barriers of the law have been removed (Rm 10:13).

By linking the Resurrection to Christ's being Lord (10:9), Paul expresses the basic inseparability between the historical Jesus and the Christ of faith. The reality of the Resurrection is related to the fact that he actually died and was buried (cf. 1 Co 15:3-5) and then appeared to those who founded the church (15:5-8). By linking faith in Jesus' Resurrection with confession that Jesus is Lord (Rm 10:9), Paul stresses the communal aspect of faith, the fact that common belief makes us members of a community of faith, mutually responsible to bear witness to one another.

We come to this faith through a succession of events which include hearing, preaching and one being sent (10:14-17). These are the works of God and they have been accomplished, as Paul shows, by appealing to the Old Testament, the law and the prophets (10:15-21). But the missing element in the chain is the one related to human response, namely, the element of faith (Rm 10:14-15). Here also Paul uses the Old Testament to show that, indeed, the word has been preached. It has gone out to the ends of the earth (10:18; cf. Ps 19:4). Preachers have been sent (Rm 10:15; cf. Is 52:7). Indeed even the "irreligious" have heard and responded (Rm 10:19; cf. Dt 32:21). But, as the prophets before Paul also warned, Israel remains a "disobedient and rebellious people" (Rm 10:21; cf. Is 65:2). Israel has yet to respond with faith.

STUDY QUESTIONS: What is the connection between "believing" and "confessing"? Why is faith not simply a private matter for Paul? Why is the Resurrection so important for Paul? What does it mean that the "word . . . is very near you"

(10:8)? How does Paul show that rejection of the gospel is a human responsibility? Is the gospel preached everywhere today?

Romans 11:1–32
ALL ISRAEL WILL BE SAVED

1,2 **11** Let me put a further question then: is it possible that God has rejected his people? Of course not. I, an Israelite, descended from Abraham through the tribe of Benjamin, ·could never agree that God had rejected his people, the people he chose specially long ago. Do you remember what scripture says of Elijah—how he complained to God 3 about Israel's behavior? ·Lord, they have killed your prophets and broken down your altars. I, and I only, remain, and they want to 4 kill me. ·What did God say to that? I have kept for myself seven thousand men who have 5 not bent the knee to Baal. ·Today the same thing has happened: there is a remnant, chosen 6 by grace. ·By grace, you notice, nothing therefore to do with good deeds, or grace would not be grace at all!

7 What follows? It was not Israel as a whole that found what it was seeking, but only the chosen few. The rest were not allowed to see 8 the truth; ·as scripture says: God has given them a sluggish spirit, unseeing eyes and inattentive ears, and they are still like that today. 9 And David says: May their own table prove a trap for them, a snare and a pitfall—let that 10 be their punishment; ·may their eyes be struck incurably blind, their backs bend for ever.

11 Let me put another question then: have the Jews fallen for ever, or have they just stumbled? Obviously they have not fallen for ever:

their fall, though, has saved the pagans in a
[12] way the Jews may now well emulate. ·Think
of the extent to which the world, the pagan
world, has benefited from their fall and defection—then think how much more it will benefit
[13] from the conversion of them all. ·Let me tell
you pagans this: I have been sent to the pagans
as their apostle, and I am proud of being sent,
[14] but the purpose of it is to make my own people
envious of you, and in this way save some of
[15] them. ·Since their rejection meant the reconciliation of the world, do you know what their
admission will mean? Nothing less than a resurrection from the dead!

[16] A whole batch of bread is made holy if the
first handful of dough is made holy; all the
[17] branches are holy if the root is holy. ·No
doubt some of the branches have been cut off,
and, like shoots of wild olive, you have been
grafted among the rest to share with them the
[18] rich sap provided by the olive tree itself, ·but
still, even if you think yourself superior to the
other branches, remember that you do not
support the root; it is the root that supports
[19] you. ·You will say, "Those branches were cut
off on purpose to let me be grafted in!" True,
[20] they were cut off, but through their unbelief;
if you still hold firm, it is only thanks to your
faith. Rather than making you proud, that
[21] should make you afraid. ·God did not spare
the natural branches, and he is not likely to
[22] spare you. ·Do not forget that God can be
severe as well as kind: he is severe to those
who fell, and he is kind to you, but only for
as long as he chooses to be, otherwise you will
[23] find yourself cut off too, ·and the Jews, if they
give up their unbelief, grafted back in your
place. God is perfectly able to graft them back
[24] again; ·after all, if you were cut from your

natural wild olive to be grafted unnaturally on to a cultivated olive, it will be much easier for them, the natural branches, to be grafted back on the tree they came from.

²⁵ There is a hidden reason for all this, brothers, of which I do not want you to be ignorant, in case you think you know more than you do. One section of Israel has become blind, but this will last only until the whole pagan ²⁶ world has entered, ·and then after this the rest of Israel will be saved as well. As scripture says: The liberator will come from Zion, he ²⁷ will banish godlessness from Jacob. ·And this is the covenant I will make with them when I take their sins away.

²⁸ The Jews are enemies of God only with regard to the Good News, and enemies only for your sake; but as the chosen people, they are still loved by God, loved for the sake of ²⁹ their ancestors. ·God never takes back his gifts or revokes his choice.

³⁰ Just as you changed from being disobedient to God, and now enjoy mercy because of their ³¹ disobedience, ·so those who are disobedient now—and only because of the mercy shown ³² to you—will also enjoy mercy eventually. ·God has imprisoned all men in their own disobedience only to show mercy to all mankind.

✠

Having surveyed the past in Romans 9 and the present in Romans 10 as part of his defense of the fidelity and justice of God, Paul considers a final challenge (11:1): "Is it possible that God has rejected his people?" The answer is an emphatic, "Of course not." Paul dismisses that eventuality conclusively by the end of Romans 11 when he commits Israel's future to the wisdom of God (11:33-36). But first he reinforces his dismissal of this possibility by presenting his own example as evidence that Israel's rejection is only *partial* (cf. 11:1-10) and then considering the inclusion of the pagans as leading to the eventual conversion of the Jews, to show that Israel's rejection is only *temporary* (11:11-32).

Paul's firm optimism about the final salvation of all Israel (11:25-26) is based on the idea of the "remnant" (11:5), which Paul borrows and adapts from Old Testament sources. The prophet Amos first introduced this idea, showing that God's fidelity would be demonstrated on the day of Yahweh when he "will take pity on the remnant of Joseph" (Am 5:15), that is, the portion of Israel who is found faithful (cf. 5:15-18). More explicitly, Paul refers to the experience of another prophet, Elijah, who alone was faithful among all the prophets of the false gods (Rm 11:2-4). Like Elijah, Paul implies, he himself represents the faithful remnant; Paul is an Israelite (11:1) who accepts the gospel which the majority of Israel rejects. Paul points to his Jewish past to emphasize that his own experience demonstrates that God is faithful to at least a remnant, "chosen by grace" (11:5). Paul will go further, showing how his own experience is both prophetic in the sense that it symbolizes a judgment against Jewish disbelief and also a cause for hope. Just as God is shown to be faithful in Paul's life, so God will be shown to be faithful in the lives of the rest of the Jews. Paul's experience shows that "today the same thing has happened" (11:5) as happened in the time of Elijah. Similarly, what is happening now is assurance for the future salvation of all. God has called Paul from life as an exemplary Jew (cf. 11:1; Ph 3:4–6) to become the apostle to the pagans (Rm 11:13). This mission is intended not only for the conversion of the pagans, but to make the Jews envious and eventually to save them (11:14).

As Paul grapples with his understanding of how God's plan for universal salvation is being effected in the history of the world, he shows himself developing and expanding a definition of Israel as the people God is saving. The meaning of Paul's assertion in 9:6 ("Not all those who descend from Israel are Israel") is further advanced in 11:26 when Paul commits to the future his faith that the "rest of Israel will be saved." The same merciful God who formerly distinguished Israel from her enemies (e.g., 9:14–18), now (but only temporarily, Paul insists) identifies the Jews as the "enemies of God only with regard to the Good News" (11:28). The confusion and suffering involved in this paradox will be resolved in the future as the "hidden reason" (11:25) of God's purpose is fully revealed for the salvation of all of Israel, the new people of God.

Paul uses numerous images to explain the paradox of Israel's rejection of the gospel. He says that Israel is blind (11:25; cf. 9:30–10:3). Only a remnant of Israel is chosen by grace (9:27, 11:5–6), whereas the majority have fallen (11:7–10; cf. 9:27–28). Yet because of Israel, the message has come to the pagans (11:11–13). By speaking of Israel as the natural as opposed to the grafted branches of the olive tree (11:16–24), Paul draws upon a traditional image in the Old Testament, though there it is usually used as relating to vines (Jr 2:21, for example). Paul and the gospel writers reflect this tradition when they define the vine as the kingdom of God (cf. Mt 20:1–8; Mk 12:1–12; Lk 20:9–19) and true Israel as the fruit of the vine (Jn 15:1–8).

Each of these images (blindness causing stumbling [Rm 11:11], the remnant chosen by grace [11:5], the natural branches and the grafted in branches [11:16–24]) helps Paul explain the present which is painful and challenging to faith in the light of the future, which is hopeful and founded upon God's fidelity. All of them have a paradoxical nature. Paul grounds his assurance that "Israel will be saved" in the mercy of God which is being revealed in the course of history as accessible to all. Nothing could be more painful to Paul than the present rejection of the gospel by the Jews. Perhaps nowhere does the Apostle manifest more strongly the conviction expressed in 8:18 that "what we suffer in this life can never be compared to the glory as yet unrevealed" than when he reconciles God's apparent rejection of the Jews with the final revelation of mercy (11:30–32). The agonized history of both Jews and the pagans is temporarily senseless and mutually exclusive, but both will be reconciled in God's mercy. God in his fidelity is forming a "new creature" (Ga 6:15), an "Israel of God" (6:16) out of the two previously hostile segments of humankind (Ep 2:13–15). Paul's vision of universal salvation allows him to catch a glimpse of the depths of the wisdom and knowledge of God which he celebrates in the hymn which brings our passage to a close (Rm 11:33–36).

Regardless of the present situation when Jews are rejecting the gospel, the scriptures make it clear that salvation comes from the Jews (Jn 4:22). Israel is God's instrument in bringing about the salvation of the world. Thus, what is happening now must be explained in terms of this aspect of the plan of God. There is a sense in which the Jews can be seen as a sacrificial people, who have become enemies of God (Rm 11:28) even as Paul himself expressed willingness to become (9:3) for the sake of the pagans' having access to the gospel. The gospel's message is that all are justified by the power of God. From this conviction, Paul argues the *need* of all to be justified. Now is when the Jews are demonstrating their need for justification, just as formerly was the time of the pagans' clear sinfulness that showed their need for justification (cf. 1:18–32).

STUDY QUESTIONS: What does Paul mean by "chosen by grace" (11:5)? Who are "the chosen few" he mentions in 11:7? Is Paul convincing when he says that God has not rejected Israel? Why? What is the mystery of God that is being revealed? Can this be revealed in the lives of individuals or only in the church? How can a person experience God's mercy because of someone else's disobedience? If God's free gift is available to all, why is Paul so intent on conversion?

Romans 11:33–36
"HOW DEEP ARE GOD'S WISDOM AND KNOWLEDGE"

³³ How rich are the depths of God—how deep his wisdom and knowledge—and how impossible to penetrate his motives or understand ³⁴ his methods! ·Who could ever know the mind of the Lord? Who could ever be his counsel- ³⁵ lor? ·Who could ever give him anything or ³⁶ lend him anything? ·All that exists comes from him; all is by him and for him. To him be glory for ever! Amen.

✠

The unfolding of God's plan for universal salvation is taking place and the plan includes all, Jews first and now the pagans. Together these form the "Israel of God" (Ga 6:16). This is a mystery involving human pain, the problem of divisions, the apparent exclusion of some for a time, limitations to total acceptance and understanding by all. God's wisdom and knowledge and power are beyond human comprehension (Rm 11:33–34). Understanding is a form of control, but faith goes beyond understanding and involves obedient acceptance. We assign meaning to our experiences in this world, but these must reflect God's values if we are to become wise. Human wisdom is submission to the wisdom of God (cf. 1:19–20). Isaiah, with the forcefulness of irony, questioned the presumption of one who would counsel God (Is 40:13; cf. Rm 11:34–35). Elsewhere in the Old Testament, the ways and thoughts of God are described as unknowable (Is 55:7–9; Ps 139:6,17–18). Only the ignorant fool would presume to advise God. But Paul has told his readers that he does not want them to be ignorant (Rm 11:25), for even in the present, in their lives and in their relationships, the "hidden reason" of God's own knowledge and wisdom is being revealed. Thus Paul concludes his contemplation on the mystery of God (i.e., the real idea behind his consideration of the meaning of Israel in Romans 9–11) with a doxology in 11:36. God's hidden purpose is being worked out in the reconciliation of pagans and Jews through the gospel, forming them both into a new creation (cf. 2 Co 5:17–20; Ga 6:15–16). God is the beginning, middle and goal of human history. Wise reasoning ends with praise. A fervent "Amen" seals Paul's act of faith.

STUDY QUESTIONS: How does Paul actually resolve the question of God's fidelity regarding Israel in Romans 9–11? For Paul, what is the mystery of God as it is being revealed in history?

Romans 12:1–16:27
PAUL'S EXHORTATIONS
TO A MIXED COMMUNITY

Paul now proceeds to the ethical exhortations that flow from the doctrinal message of the first part of this epistle. In a sense, 12:1 could appropriately follow 8:39 according to the indicative-imperative structure that is basic to Paul's epistles generally. But the Apostle inserted his reflections on the extremely painful problem involving Israel's rejection of the gospel in Romans 9–11 which seemed to interrupt this structure. While not furnishing sufficient information to give us a really concrete picture of the community at Rome, 12:1–16:27 does prove to be most fertile for helping Christians build good relationships within a mixed community and engender peace with the outside world. At the same time, Paul shares his own plans, his vision of his ministry and his apparent affection for his readers in these chapters.

In 12:1–21, Paul describes the relationships between individuals within the community, using the Greek image of the commonwealth as a body. In 13:1–7, he turns to the relationship of Christians to the State, and in 13:8–14 he reminds his readers of the coming of the time of salvation. Tolerance of others, Paul goes on to say in 14:1–15:6, transcends all personal differences. In 15:7–33, Paul appears ready to close the letter, appealing for unity (15:7-13) and describing his ministry plans which involve visiting the Romans (15:14-33). Romans 16 seems to be a kind of appendix where Paul greets his friends and warns those troubling the community; he concludes with a hymn of praise.

In general, then, it is notable that Paul's reflections in 12:1-16:27 represent concrete applications to issues of community and ministry or the doctrinal basics he developed in 1:1-8:39.

Romans 12:1–21
THE COMMUNITY AS A BODY

¹ 12 Think of God's mercy, my brothers, and worship him, I beg you, in a way that is worthy of thinking beings, by offering your living bodies as a holy sacrifice, truly ² pleasing to God. ·Do not model yourselves on the behavior of the world around you, but let your behavior change, modeled by your new mind. This is the only way to discover the will of God and know what is good, what it is that God wants, what is the perfect thing to do.

³ In the light of the grace I have received I want to urge each one among you not to exaggerate his real importance. Each of you must judge himself soberly by the standard of the ⁴ faith God has given him. ·Just as each of our bodies has several parts and each part has a ⁵ separate function, ·so all of us, in union with Christ, form one body, and as parts of it we ⁶ belong to each other. ·Our gifts differ according to the grace given us. If your gift is prophecy, then use it as your faith suggests; ⁷ if administration, then use it for administra- ⁸ tion; if teaching, then use it for teaching. ·Let the preachers deliver sermons, the almsgivers give freely, the officials be diligent, and those who do works of mercy do them cheerfully.

⁹ Do not let your love be a pretense, but sin- ¹⁰ cerely prefer good to evil. ·Love each other as much as brothers should, and have a pro- ¹¹ found respect for each other. ·Work for the

Lord with untiring effort and with great earnestness of spirit. ·If you have hope, this will make you cheerful. Do not give up if trials come; and keep on praying. ·If any of the saints are in need you must share with them; and you should make hospitality your special care.

¹⁴ Bless those who persecute you: never curse them, bless them. ·Rejoice with those who rejoice and be sad with those in sorrow. ·Treat everyone with equal kindness; never be condescending but make real friends with the poor. Do not allow yourself to become self-satisfied. ·Never repay evil with evil but let everyone see that you are interested only in the highest ideals. ·Do all you can to live at peace with everyone. ·Never try to get revenge; leave that, my friends, to God's anger. As scripture says: Vengeance is mine—I will pay them back, the Lord promises. ·But there is more: If your enemy is hungry, you should give him food, and if he is thirsty, let him drink. Thus you heap red-hot coals on his head. ·Resist evil and conquer it with good.

☩

Christian imperatives result from faith. All Christian actions and relationships such as Paul describes in 12:1–15:13 should be reflections inspired by the mercy of God (12:1). The image of the body (12:4–6), probably borrowed by Paul from the Stoic notion of the commonwealth, expresses the primacy of the love which must provide the basic Christian motivation. Christians must not only be inspired by the example of Christ, but show true love by their union with Christ (12:5). They must place their gifts at the service of the body, for the good of the church (12:6-8; 1 Co 12:12-30). Thus there can be no competition or jealousy among Christians (cf. Rm 12:3; Ph 2:1-4) who derive a "new mind" (Rm 12:2) from Christ. In like manner, Paul instructed the Philippians, "In your minds you must be the same as Christ Jesus" (Ph 2:5).

Paul's exhortation to live, worthy of God's call and gift, in Christ proceeds from the faith he described in Romans 1-8. Paul's language, especially in 12:1-2 (cf. 1:9: "The God I worship spiritually" and 15:16: "I am to carry out my priestly duty by bringing the Good News from God to the pagans, and so make them acceptable as an offering, made holy by the Holy Spirit"), reflects the liturgical setting in which Paul probably envisioned his words would be read to the Christians assembled in Roman houses in celebration of the Eucharist or Baptism. Paul admonishes them that their entire lives are a living sacrifice as a result of reflecting on God's mercy (12:1). The following list of instructions could be staggering if we forget that for Paul every action is subordinate to the one essential of love. This theme is evident in the image of the body which helps explain the Christians' interdependence. And Paul punctuates the chapter with reminders of this theme. In 12:9, for example, he says, "Do not let your love be a pretense," and in 12:14, he encourages the Christians to "bless those who persecute you."

Paul enjoins the Roman Christians to offer spiritual worship to God (12:1-2) through a life of service and community (12:3–21). Paul describes the relationship among individual Christians as based on love which enables them to put their gifts at the service of the community. The community is represented by the image of the body (12:4–5). Not only within the community (12:6–13), but with outsiders (12:14–21) relationships must reflect the primacy of love.

Paul alludes to the saying of Jesus found in Luke's gospel: "Be compassionate as your Father is compassionate" (Lk 6:36), rooting his admonitions not in human power but in the mercy of God (Rm 12:1–2). The Apostle reminds the Romans that this compassion is not limited to other members of the Christian community but extends even to their persecutors (Rm 12:14; cf. Mt 5:44). Paul seems to be aware of the tradition ascribed to Jesus' saying: "You have learned how it was said, Eye for eye and tooth for tooth. But I say this to you: offer the wicked . . . no resistance. On the contrary, if anyone hits you on the right cheek, offer him the other as well" (5:38–39). In other words, Christian ethics require that the believer not retaliate (Rm 12:17), but sincerely "prefer good to evil" (12:9), resisting evil and conquering it with good (12:21). Thus, the measure of love in action is the way one behaves toward one's persecutors or toward the poor (12:14–16), the common denominator between these groups being their unwillingness or inability to reciprocate in kind.

STUDY QUESTIONS: Do you agree with Paul that the only way to discover the will of

God and what is good is to surrender your being completely to God? If so, what does this involve? What are some implications of subsuming all things under hospitality and making that your special concern (12:13)? Paul describes the community as a body; what implications does that image have for us today when there are many communities which profess faith in Jesus? Since we are not to act in a vengeful way, what does one do with anger and resentment? Is Paul realistic?

Romans 13:1–7
THE CHRISTIAN AND THE STATE

¹ 13 You must all obey the governing authorities. Since all government comes from God, the civil authorities were appointed ² by God, ·and so anyone who resists authority is rebelling against God's decision, and such ³ an act is bound to be punished. ·Good behavior is not afraid of magistrates; only criminals have anything to fear. If you want to live without being afraid of authority, you must live honestly and authority may even honor you. ⁴ The state is there to serve God for your benefit. If you break the law, however, you may well have fear: the bearing of the sword has its significance. The authorities are there to serve God: they carry out God's revenge by ⁵ punishing wrongdoers. ·You must obey, therefore, not only because you are afraid of being ⁶ punished, but also for conscience' sake. ·This is also the reason why you must pay taxes, since all government officials are God's offi- ⁷ cers. They serve God by collecting taxes. ·Pay every government official what he has a right to ask—whether it be direct tax or indirect, fear or honor.

✠

Paul's comments in 13:1–7 about the Christians' relationship to the state must be understood within the limits of his attempt to encourage a struggling minority group dominated by a powerful, hostile government. Paul warns the Christians that they may not flee or oppose or even undermine the human institution of the state but recognize it as the instrument of God. Since government exercises the power of God, it is in some way condoned by God and, therefore, God's instrument. Paul does not challenge the form of, justice of or alternatives to the state's use of power. Nor does he deal with the question of the abuse of power. The fact that God lets it be necessitates that the state be respected by the Christians.

The problems facing Christians as Roman citizens were exacerbated by their conversion, not diminished. Nor were their problems limited to simply learning to relate to one another as members of the community or to developing a tolerant attitude toward their persecutors (cf. 12:9–21). They were particularly vulnerable vis-à-vis the state and it is understandable that this would have been an acute issue with the community of Rome. There the concentrated power of the state continually represented a potential threat to the independence of religion. Indeed, ancient Rome with its cult of the Emperor tolerated only with difficulty the least expression of separating religion and state. Unwillingness to participate in the cult of the Emperor came to be interpreted as treason. Rome remained vigilant, especially toward the Jews. It judged them difficult to control, primarily because the Jews insisted upon at least a modicum of independence of religion. New Testament evidence attests at times to Rome's rather impatient attitude toward the Jews who had their own law, and the growth of Christianity did not ease these tensions but aggravated them. The Emperor Claudius, for example, according to the historian Suetonius, expelled the Jews from Rome in A.D. 49 on account of riots which arose at the instigation of "Chrestus," generally presumed to be a mistaken reference to Christ; apparently Roman authorities were not able to make a distinction between Judaism and nascent Christianity. The fact that the Emperor expelled the Jews because of riots over Christ indicates the extent to which minority religions, particularly Judaism, were at the mercy of the state. It is important, also, to remember that the Jews who would have lived in Rome probably had been brought there as captives, servants, workers, even slaves of the Roman masters. The expulsion of the Jews from Rome shortly before Paul's letter was written would have served as a powerful reminder to the Christian community which Paul addressed of their vulnerability in a hostile state.

Paul is not alone among the New Testament writers in concerning himself with this intricate problem of the relation between the Christians and the state. Clearly the problem had several dimensions. On the more negative side, Paul exhorts the Christians not to rock the boat. Common sense prompts the Apostle to suggest that they do not attract undue attention from a hostile state that threatened their very existence. On the positive side, Paul encourages them in the obligations they have as citizens. The Apostle takes the position that Baptism is not to be used as a convenient escape from the obligations of living in the world. In other contexts, when Christians attempted to use their conversion as an excuse to detach themselves from marriage (1 Co 7:1–11), for example, or from ordinary work (2 Th 3:6–12), Paul admonishes them to continue to carry out the responsibilities they already had at the time of their conversion (1 Co 7:17). Ever the pastor, Paul recognizes the difficulties involved in being faithful, but he encourages the Christians not to flee the world but to participate actively in such human institutions as marriage and the obligations of citizenship.

Some Christians today might be disappointed that Paul does not provide more helpful guidance for the complicated issues involved in responsible citizenship which could include conscientious objection or civil disobedience. But in Paul's day the delicate balance between minority religions and a hostile state was difficult to maintain, and upsetting it could have threatened the very survival of Christianity. The early church was almost overwhelmed by the identity struggle it was engaged in vis-à-vis both Judaism and Rome. The world of the New Testament made little distinction between politics and religion. If Christians resisted the state, they risked being crushed in the process. In a world where patriotism included participation in the cult of the Emperor and refusal implied treason, Paul's exhortation to the Roman Christians to give officials the minimum of what they "have a right to ask" is almost revolutionary. The Christian conscience, Paul says, supports these rights (Rm 13:5). But, as Paul will go on to say in the next section, the Christians' obligations toward one another are far more demanding. Love is the debt they owe each other (13:8–9), whereas all they owe their officials are taxes, fear and honor (13:7).

STUDY QUESTIONS: Do you agree that "all government comes from God" (13:1)? What could this mean to us? Is there any place for civil disobedience if this statement is part of scripture? What does Paul mean by "law" here (13:4)?

Romans 13:8–14
"THE 'TIME' HAS COME"

8 Avoid getting into debt, except the debt of mutual love. If you love your fellow men you
9 have carried out your obligations. ·All the commandments: You shall not commit adultery, you shall not kill, you shall not steal, you shall not covet, and so on, are summed up in this single command: You must love
10 your neighbor as yourself. ·Love is the one thing that cannot hurt your neighbor; that is why it is the answer to every one of the commandments.
11 Besides, you know "the time" has come: you must wake up now: our salvation is even nearer than it was when we were converted.
12 The night is almost over, it will be daylight soon—let us give up all the things we prefer to do under cover of the dark; let us arm our-
13 selves and appear in the light. ·Let us live decently as people do in the daytime: no drunken orgies, no promiscuity or licentious-
14 ness, and no wrangling or jealousy. ·Let your armor be the Lord Jesus Christ; forget about satisfying your bodies with all their cravings.

☩

The core of Paul's ethical considerations, the hub to which all of his individual exhortations must be connected, is stated in 13:8–10, which simply sums up morality as love. The only thing that cannot hurt another, Paul says, is love (13:10) and all of the other commandments forbid hurting others. It is Paul who originates the idea of love being the "debt" Christians owe one another (13:8; cf. 15:27). Repaying the debt of love, then, by taking care of one another testifies to Christians' acceptance of the gospel (cf. 1 Co 9:11–14; Ga 6:2,6). Paul implies that we can only give what we have been given. Our acceptance of the gift of love makes us indebted to one another. The gospel of Luke also describes love as a duty expressed in almsgiving and in the care of the needy (Lk 6:30,35,38, 11:41, 12:33).

In the course of Paul's ethical considerations since the beginning of Romans 12, he has included the most negative relationships (e.g., revenge; Rm 12:19, 13:4), as well as common wisdom about relationships within a hostile state (13:1–7). Now Paul reveals love as the foundation of all the Christian's relationships and the basis of all moral obligation. Paul and the tradition of the Gospels show that the challenge and the uniqueness of Christianity lies in the simplicity of its uncompromising identification with love of God, love of neighbor and love of self. (This is the significance of the terms "all" and "summed up" in 13:9). As the one thing that cannot hurt your neighbor, love is the answer to every one of God's commandments. Similarly, when Jesus was "tested" by students of the law who asked him which was the greatest commandment (Mt 22:34–40; Mk 12:28–31; cf. Lk 10:25–28), he silenced his questioners (Mk 12:34) not so much because his answer was so brilliant, but because it was so clear and simple.

The Gospels repeatedly record illustrations of how would-be followers were intellectually comprehending but unwilling to pay the high cost of discipleship, described as the debt of love, required of one who took Jesus at his word—the one who wished to go first and bury his father (Lk 9:59–60), the rich young man (18:18–23), the hearers of the "bread of life" discourse who found his sayings too much for them and so no longer walked with him (Jn 6:59–66). Rabbinic teaching held that the smallest part of the law was equivalent to the largest in binding effect. Fervent Jews recited daily the words, "Listen, Israel: Yahweh our God is the one Yahweh. You shall love Yahweh your God with all your heart, with all your soul, with all your strength" (Dt 6:4–5). Rabbinic teaching also, like Christianity, tended to see Lv 19:18 ("Love your neighbor as yourself") as a kind of summary of the other commandments. But it was Jesus who joined the truth of Dt 6:4–5 to Lv 19:18 and made them equivalent. By doing so, he opposed the possibility of reducing justice or true worship of God to a mere observance of the law. And he condemned any religious act that would be contrary to tolerance or love (cf. Rm 14:1–15:6, below).

Paul packs 13:11–14 with images the early church used to describe its life of faith. The "time," Paul writes, has come (cf. 2 Co 6:2; Mk 1:15, 13:33; Lk 21:8; Jn 7:6 and passim). Jesus cautioned his disciples that the "time" (i.e., the *kairos*, the opportune moment, referring in the Gospels to the Passion or to the last judgment) approached like a burglar at night (e.g., Mt 24:43; Lk 12:39). Daylight is replacing the night, Paul says (Rm 13:12); and John's gospel, especially, is full of the contrasting night-day, darkness-light images (e.g., Jn 1:4 and passim). Awakened from the sleep of sin, the Christian is called to watchful awareness, a heightened sensitivity, like one alert to do battle against a strong enemy (Rm 13:14). Similarly, Jesus, before the Passion warned his disciples to watch and to be on guard (Mt 24:42–43, 25:13; Mk 13:33–37).

According to Paul, as human beings we are under the powerful spiritual forces of either death or life. Evil threatens to seduce, drug, desensitize us. The common denominator of the sins Paul lists in Rm 13:13 is that these all divert us from the Christian vision of faith. They are futile attempts to satisfy self-centered cravings while they strip us of the protective defenses of vigilance, mutual commitment, forgiving love.

The awakening Paul describes is progressive (13:11). Salvation is the goal of human existence. Jesus began the work of salvation by reconciling us to God through the justification of the cross (cf. Rm 5:6–11). Now our salvation is nearer. Now is the day of salvation, Paul says (2 Co 6:2). Now we work out our salvation "in fear and trembling" (Ph 2:12). Our previous existence under sin is described in terms of darkness, sleep, debauchery, aimlessness (Rm 13:13–14). What we did formerly is opposed to our life now in Christ (6:19–21, 8:1–2, 11:30–31; Ga 1:23, 2:20, 4:9). The Christian draws not only encouragement but power from

Christ. Faith equips him or her with the "armor" of Christ (Rm 13:14). As one grows in Christ the as yet unredeemed aspects of our lives are surrendered to Jesus' Lordship and we draw nearer to the fullness of salvation. This gives meaning to the "time" assigned to us and especially to the present, the now which is ours.

The Gospels describe the Passion of Jesus as the "hour" of fulfillment (cf. Mk 14:41; Lk 22:53; Jn 17:1). Something of the same connotation of fulfillment is involved in Paul's challenge to awaken *now* (Rm 13:13). "Now" is more than a passing time between the past and the present. It is the moment ripe with challenge to participate in proclaiming Jesus as Lord. It is a moment to overcome the lethargy of sin and experience being fully alive to God.

STUDY QUESTIONS: If the commandment to love one's neighbor is the summation and the greatest commandment, do we need and why do we have others? Is the love command too simple? What does Paul mean by " 'the time' has come . . . salvation is even nearer than it was when we were converted" (13:11)? What are some signs of this? What do you understand by the "night" that is almost over (13:12)?

Romans 14:1 – 15:6
THE "STRONG" AND THE "WEAK" IN COMMUNITY

1 14 If a person's faith is not strong enough, welcome him all the same without start-
2 ing an argument. ·People range from those who believe they may eat any sort of meat to those whose faith is so weak they dare not
3 eat anything except vegetables. ·Meat eaters must not despise the scrupulous. On the other hand, the scrupulous must not condemn those who feel free to eat anything they choose, since
4 God has welcomed them. ·It is not for you to condemn someone else's servant: whether he stands or falls it is his own master's business; he will stand, you may be sure, because the
5 Lord has power to make him stand. ·If one man keeps certain days as holier than others, and another considers all days to be equally holy, each must be left free to hold his own
6 opinion. ·The one who observes special days does so in honor of the Lord. The one who eats meat also does so in honor of the Lord, since he gives thanks to God; but then the man who abstains does that too in honor of the
7 Lord, and so he also gives God thanks. ·The life and death of each of us has its influence
8 on others; ·if we live, we live for the Lord; and if we die, we die for the Lord, so that
9 alive or dead we belong to the Lord. ·This explains why Christ both died and came to life, it was so that he might be Lord both of
10 the dead and of the living. ·This is also why

you should never pass judgment on a brother
or treat him with contempt, as some of you
have done. We shall have to stand before the
¹¹ judgment seat of God; ·as scripture says: By
my life—it is the Lord who speaks—every knee
¹² shall bend before ·me, and every tongue shall
praise God. It is to God, therefore, that each
of us must give an account of himself.

¹³ Far from passing judgment on each other,
therefore, you should make up your mind
never to be the cause of your brother tripping
¹⁴ or falling. ·Now I am perfectly well aware,
of course, and I speak for the Lord Jesus, that
no food is unclean in itself; however, if someone thinks that a particular food is unclean,
¹⁵ then it is unclean for him. ·And indeed if your
attitude to food is upsetting your brother, then
you are hardly being guided by charity. You
are certainly not free to eat what you like if
that means the downfall of someone for whom
Christ died.

¹⁶ In short, you must not compromise your
¹⁷ privilege, ·because the kingdom of God does
not mean eating or drinking this or that, it
means righteousness and peace and joy brought
¹⁸ by the Holy Spirit. ·If you serve Christ in this
way you will please God and be respected by
¹⁹ men. ·So let us adopt any custom that leads to
²⁰ peace and our mutual improvement; ·do not
wreck God's work over a question of food. Of
course all food is clean, but it becomes evil if
by eating it you make somebody else fall away.
²¹ In such cases the best course is to abstain from
meat and wine and anything else that would
make your brother trip or fall or weaken in
any way.

²² Hold on to your own belief, as between
yourself and God—and consider the man for-
tunate who can make his decision without go-

²³ ing against his conscience. ·But anybody who eats in a state of doubt is condemned, because he is not in good faith; and every act done in bad faith is a sin.

15 ¹ We who are strong have a duty to put up with the qualms of the weak without ² thinking of ourselves. ·Each of us should think of his neighbors and help them to become ³ stronger Christians. ·Christ did not think of himself: the words of scripture—the insults of those who insult you fall on me—apply to him. ⁴ And indeed everything that was written long ago in the scriptures was meant to teach us something about hope from the examples scripture gives of how people who did not give ⁵ up were helped by God. ·And may he who helps us when we refuse to give up, help you all to be tolerant with each other, following ⁶ the example of Christ Jesus, ·so that united in mind and voice you may give glory to the God and Father of our Lord Jesus Christ.

✠

Whereas Romans 12 and 13 seemed to concentrate on the contributions and obligations of individuals within the community, 14:1–15:6 focus on the community as a whole and the possible divisions that threaten it. The reasons Paul gives for these divisions might seem remote for some of us. The Apostle speaks of the vegetarians (14:2) in tension with the meat eaters (14:3), of those who celebrate certain feasts at odds with those who consider all days to be equally holy (14:5–6). Yet, very simple adaptation of Paul's examples could make this passage relevant today as a paradigm for any group of people divided on issues concerning life together. Paul recognizes that tensions do exist even within a community renowned for its faith (1:8, 15:14). Perhaps he refers to real divisions in Rome based on reports he has heard or questions that community raised. Others have spoken about that community and he seems to be so satisfied with it that he felt no need to write primarily for the sake of settling differences, as he had to do when writing the Thessalonians and the Corinthians, for example. More probably Paul surmised that the Roman Christians, as a mixed community composed of former Jews and pagans, the latter probably being in the majority there, would have experienced problems comparable to those encountered by communities Paul did know and advise personally. It would have made sense, then, to give the Romans the benefit of his experience. Thus, as he brings the letter to a close, Paul encouraged the Roman Christians to rely on tolerance to overcome their personal differences (14:7–15), "following the example of Christ Jesus" (15:5).

In 14:1–15:6, Paul addresses both those who are "strong" and those who are "weak." These comments can best be understood in the light of the love command expressed in 13:9–10. In essence, Paul agrees with those of "strong" faith whose freedom in Christ allows them to disregard the laws and ordinances Jesus overcame by his death. Yet, Paul contends, individual faith, freedom and preferred customs are all subordinate to love, which Jesus not only commands us to live by but enables us to live by. "Conscience" in the New Testament is a Pauline term that is frequently not understood because what it stands for is considered autonomous, isolated, individual (see discussion of 2:1–29, p. 143).

We are all subject to God's judgment (14:10), Paul writes. Therefore Christians must refrain from judging one another lest they be judged according to their own merits and condemned. Nor can Christians scandalize each other, causing one to fall for whom Christ died (14:13). Nor may they reject one another because of differences of opinion regarding lifestyle or what is right or wrong (14:10–15). Rather, Christian judgment must be based on love and tolerance. That is why God's justice, as Christ revealed it, is also mercy. The strong are obliged to consider that, like themselves, the weak are those for whom Christ died (14:15). Love is given to all. It is the only universal and absolute value of the gospel. Therefore, tolerance, having itself no limits, regulates and subordinates individual consciences and action (15:1–6). To judge or to reject another on the basis of ethical or liturgical differences is to risk being ourselves outside the judgment of love by which and for which we are judged and become accountable to one another. Christian life, for Paul, is opposed to the idea that one may simply follow one's own conscience. Rather, as Paul says, "The life and death of each of us has its influence on others" (14:7).

Conscience in Paul always has this communal context to qualify its meaning. This context is essential for understanding 14:22–23. Paraphrased, Paul is saying that the faith that is "between yourself and

God" is expressed in community. Community—that is, mutual love—is the essence of faith and the expression of faith, Paul explains in 14:1–15:6. From the Christian perspective, then, at issue is not only whether the "weak" or the "strong" are correct; the consciences of both are subject to the law of love and their judgments must be tested in love. Consider faith, then, Paul says, as God's gift and imitate the person who does not violate this gift either in himself or in others, for anyone who does not act out of love, sins.

STUDY QUESTIONS: Does Paul think that dietary laws are important? What is the role of the Holy Spirit in reconciling disputes in the community? How is it that people can hold different beliefs and still be acceptable to God, still be members of one community? Do disputes destroy the possibility of community? What are some of the disagreements in our own day analogous to those that disturbed the Romans? What is the meaning of "faith" in this passage? Who are the "strong" and the "weak"?

Romans 15:7–13
A CALL FOR UNITY

⁷ It can only be to God's glory, then, for you to treat each other in the same friendly way ⁸ as Christ treated you. ·The reason Christ became the servant of circumcised Jews was not only so that God could faithfully carry out the ⁹ promises made to the patriarchs, ·it was also to get the pagans to give glory to God for his mercy, as scripture says in one place: For this I shall praise you among the pagans and sing ¹⁰ to your name. ·And in another place: Rejoice, ¹¹ pagans, with his people, ·and in a third place: Let all the pagans praise the Lord, let all the ¹² peoples sing his praises. ·Isaiah too has this to say: The root of Jesse will appear, rising up to rule the pagans, and in him the pagans will put their hope.

¹³ May the God of hope bring you such joy and peace in your faith that the power of the Holy Spirit will remove all bounds to hope.

✠

As the main part of Paul's letter to the Romans draws to a close, it is typical of him to make an appeal for unity, especially since he has just reflected on the real or potential threats of divisions among the Christians he addresses (14:1–15:6). At first it may seem that Paul demands the impossible, namely, that all follow the example of Christ (15:7). But it must be remembered that Christ is far more than a model for Christians. It is by Christ that the community is created and that Christians are able to love one another.

Christ breaks down the barriers not only between God and people (cf. 5:2,8-11, 8:3-4) but also between people. This is what Paul means when he says in Ep 2:13-14: "You that used to be so far apart . . . have been brought very close . . . [Christ] is the peace between us." It was the law that used to separate God's chosen ones from the pagan sinners. Now Christ has broken down this barrier (cf. Rm 10:4) and enabled all to live in peace. Through Christ, the pagans and the Jews alike have received the promise of God's mercy (10:12). Because of Christ, there are no more limits to hope, no limits to reconciliation (15:13).

STUDY QUESTIONS: Paul seems to want everyone to come together in God. Is this really possible? Does this mean that everyone should think alike? When we consider the reconciliation Jesus won for us, do we reflect on the limits we set in our relationships with each other? Should we? What are the limits to our hope, individual and collective? Do you believe that Christ can remove them?

Romans 15:14–21
THE APOSTLE OPENS HIS HEART

¹⁴ It is not because I have any doubts about you, my brothers; on the contrary I am quite certain that you are full of good intentions, perfectly well instructed and able to advise ¹⁵ each other. ·The reason why I have written to you, and put some things rather strongly, is to refresh your memories, since God has given ¹⁶ me this special position. ·He has appointed me as a priest of Jesus Christ, and I am to carry out my priestly duty by bringing the Good News from God to the pagans, and so make them acceptable as an offering, made holy by the Holy Spirit.

¹⁷ I think I have some reason to be proud of what I, in union with Christ Jesus, have been ¹⁸ able to do for God. ·What I am presuming to speak of, of course, is only what Christ himself has done to win the allegiance of the pa- ¹⁹ gans, using what I have said and done ·by the power of signs and wonders, by the power of the Holy Spirit. Thus, all the way along, from Jerusalem to Illyricum, I have preached Christ's Good News to the utmost of my ca- ²⁰ pacity. ·I have always, however, made it an unbroken rule never to preach where Christ's name has already been heard. The reason for that was that I had no wish to build on other ²¹ men's foundations; ·on the contrary, my chief concern has been to fulfill the text: Those who have never been told about him will see him,

and those who have never heard about him will understand.

☩

In 15:14–21, drawing on language from the liturgy, Paul describes his ministry (15:16). Yet his "priestly" ministry is not carried out at an altar nor in a church or synagogue. His is a worldwide mission. As God's "priest" (this translation for the Greek *leitourgos* is not really satisfactory since today it connotes a very different role than the one Paul played; a "liturgist" originally performed some kind of public service), Paul is appointed to bring about the allegiance of the pagans to the gospel (15:16–19). The Apostle speaks and the pagans hear because the action of God through the Holy Spirit has brought them together (15:18–19). Paul's mission to the pagans is his "liturgy."

Since he is so aware that only through the gospel is such total communication achieved, Paul can speak of his pride in his apostolate (15:17). Although human boasts based on pride are excluded and condemned as obstacles to faith (1 Co 1:29; Ep 2:8–9), Paul not only condones, he encourages boasting about the Lord (cf. his quotation of Jr 9:22–23 in 1 Co 1:31 and 2 Co 10:17). Real communication, when truth aids people to come to loving unity, can only be achieved through the Spirit. This unity is the great sign of the presence of the Spirit. Acts tells us of miraculous deeds Paul performs (e.g., Ac 14:8–10, 19:11–17), but Paul himself does not speak of any miracles he worked except this reference in Rm 15:19. Yet Paul does describe his primary function as an Apostle as preaching (15:16; 1 Co 1:17), and this function helps create community based on faith in the gospel he preaches. It would be consistent with Paul's theology of vocation and mission, as well as with his constant encouragement to community, for us to interpret the "signs and wonders" of Rm 15:19 in the context of how he has helped create community. There is no greater sign of hope than community and no greater wonder than that community is possible, transcending all divisions such as he just described (14:1–15:6).

Paul's statement in 15:20 about his "unbroken rule" of never preaching where the name of Christ "has already been heard" seems surprising—maybe even contradictory to the very existence of this letter to a community he has not founded. Why, then, we might ask, did he write to the Romans? This question probably does not have a simple, one-dimensional response. The apparent contradiction here suggests that Paul's reasons for writing were complex, like the Apostle himself. As capital of the civilized world, Rome represents an obvious target for Paul's universal apostolic mission. As "Apostle to the pagans," he could not help but be attracted by the challenge of that famous pagan city. Yet going to Rome, the city that symbolized the power that put Jesus to death and threatened Christians with the same fate, could mean the end of Paul's own ministry. Or, as Paul hoped, Rome could be the gateway to Spain (15:23–24,28) and the Christians in

Rome could provide the necessary respite Paul needed to refresh his mission.

The twin aspects of Rome's challenge and its threat to Paul accounts, at least partially, for the ambivalence Paul seems to feel in writing despite his personal resolve never to preach where Christ's name is already known (15:20). Many other instances can be found where Paul insists that personal preferences, opinions or values have to be subordinated to the demands of the gospel. Yet it is not hard to understand Paul's ambivalence. Traces of it are already apparent in Paul's introduction in 1:8–15, including the words: "I am longing to see you either to strengthen you by sharing a spiritual gift with you, or what is better, to find encouragement among you from our common faith" (1:11–12). Clearly, Paul is writing to these Christians, not simply to "build on other men's foundations" (15:20) nor even just to preach, inform or introduce himself or his gospel.

Paul's reasons for writing, like his reasons for visiting Rome soon, are many. They include his being ministered to by being able to share his gospel reflections with the Romans, as well as being himself able to minister to them. The urgency of the gospel to him supersedes any personal resolutions about the limits of the territory in which he will preach. As Paul states more explicitly in 15:24–28, his eyes are fixed on Spain. He will not deny himself or the Romans the mutual, strengthening encouragement that a letter followed by a visit will mean.

STUDY QUESTIONS: What does Paul mean when he

refers to making the pagans "acceptable as an offering" (15:16)? Paul refers to himself as a "priest" of Jesus Christ; what does he mean by this? What are some present-day examples of "priestly" duties that could be similar to Paul's? Is it more important to preach the gospel to those who have never heard it than to continue to teach and challenge those who already profess to be Christians?

Romans 15:22–33
THE APOSTLE ASKS FOR PRAYERS

²² That is the reason why I have been kept
²³ from visiting you so long, ·though for many years I have been longing to pay you a visit. Now, however, having no more work to do
²⁴ here, ·I hope to see you on my way to Spain and, after enjoying a little of your company, to complete the rest of the journey with your
²⁵ good wishes. ·First, however, I must take a present of money to the saints in Jerusalem,
²⁶ since Macedonia and Achaia have decided to send a generous contribution to the poor
²⁷ among the saints at Jerusalem. ·A generous contribution as it should be, since it is really repaying a debt: the pagans who share the spiritual possessions of these poor people have a duty to help them with temporal possessions.
²⁸ So when I have done this and officially handed over what has been raised, I shall set out for
²⁹ Spain and visit you on the way. ·I know that when I reach you I shall arrive with rich blessings from Christ.

³⁰ But I beg you, brothers, by our Lord Jesus Christ and the love of the Spirit, to help me through my dangers by praying to God for me.
³¹ Pray that I may escape the unbelievers in Judaea, and that the aid I carry to Jerusalem may
³² be accepted by the saints. ·Then, if God wills, I shall be feeling very happy when I come to
³³ enjoy a period of rest among you. ·May the God of peace be with you all! Amen.

✠

Despite the resolution (15:20) that so far has kept Paul away from Rome (since there were still many lands that had not yet been evangelized), Paul feels compelled to visit the Christian community there, to bolster them and himself, on his way to the distant land of Spain (15:24,28). In those days of Roman domination of the world, all roads did indeed lead to Rome. The challenge of far-off pagan Spain must have beckoned Paul like the haunting voice of the Macedonian in Paul's vision, who appealed to Paul, "Come . . . and help us" (Ac 16:9). Paul embarked on his first missionary journey in response to this voice, which he interpreted as revealing the will of God. Now he feels called to continue his mission all the way to Spain, which represented the uttermost boundaries of the world. The course of Paul's ministry to Spain was naturally set so as to include Rome.

Now only one errand remains standing between the Apostle and the fulfillment of this goal—namely, the delivery of the money contributed by Greek communities to Jerusalem (15:25–28). It is possible to fail to see the extreme importance of this contribution, either in itself or in view of the sense of urgency Paul seems to feel about delivering it in person. Yet essential to appreciating Paul's mentality in writing Romans and his delay in visiting them until now, is understanding how important a symbol the collection of money was and what this symbol meant to Paul and to the first-century church.

To say that the contribution was a "symbol" is not to detract from its real value or from the importance of Paul's efforts to raise it (cf. 2 Co 8:1–9:15). In fact, it would be hard to overestimate the value Paul placed on his churches' making significant monetary contributions. Paul feared that the pagans he worked with were looked upon and treated by the Jewish Christians—even their leaders— as second-class citizens. Perhaps the Jewish Christians suspected that the pagans' faith was still superficial, insufficiently deep to involve real ethical commitment. The pagans, or at least the Greeks, were noted for divorcing spirit from matter, and thus they were susceptible to such intellectualizing tendencies as Gnosticism, for example, that claimed that religion was enlightenment and that ethics or behavior was insignificant. Paul had to spend a lot of time and energy overcoming this bias against the pagans, convincing the pagans themselves that belief must be manifest in practice and convincing the Jewish Christians that the pagans' faith was as firm and as practical as their own.

During the late fifties, there was a famine in Jerusalem that affected many. The mother church there was literally starving and in need, and, by comparison, the pagan Christians had a surplus of food and money. Paul, characteristically, sees this as an opportunity for the spread and acceptance of the gospel. The pagans' aid to the Jerusalem saints (Rm 15:31) can be a lesson to both. The pagans have come to believe in Jesus, a faith shared with the

Jewish Christians. Christ came into the world through the Jews (9:5). But because of the Jewish rejection of the gospel, pagans have shared in the salvation Christ brought (11:11–13). Therefore, Paul argues, the pagans are indebted to the Jews (15:27).

It is inconceivable that the pagan Christians, having thus shared the highest spiritual blessings (i.e., faith), would be unwilling to share the less significant material goods with the Jewish Christians (15:27; 1 Co 9:11). The size of the pagans' offering aptly illustrates their degree of indebtedness; significantly, it is no small amount they send. Acceptance of this sharing (Rm 15:31) by the Jewish Christians, especially those in Jerusalem, would, in turn, represent their conversion from former suspicions to a willing acknowledgment of the pagans' full partnership in the gospel. Further, Paul is suggesting, acceptance of the pagans' contribution by the Jerusalem authorities would represent the Jerusalem community's recognition and support of the pagan mission. It would also probably mean that Paul could enlist their aid in protecting himself against "the unbelievers in Judea" (15:31; cf. also Ac 20:3,22–23, 21:13).

The contribution, then, symbolizes acceptance of Paul's mission and the reconciliation of pagans and Jews in the gospel. It also represents mutual indebtedness, overcoming pride. It implies generosity and humility and even danger. Paul identifies the contribution with himself and with his gospel. Thus, it is urgent that he is accompanied by the prayers of the Roman Christians not only for his own personal safety but for the symbolic value the contribution represents.

STUDY QUESTIONS: What is the significance of the contribution of the pagan Christians? Does Paul exaggerate the importance of money? Why would the Jewish Christians in Jerusalem refuse the gift if they needed it? What does Paul mean by saying the contribution is the pagans' "debt"? Does Paul mean that we are obliged to give money to the church?

Romans 16:1–16
GREETINGS AND MORE

¹⁶ ¹ I commend to you our sister Phoebe, a deaconess of the church at Cenchreae. ² Give her, in union with the Lord, a welcome worthy of saints, and help her with anything she needs: she has looked after a great many people, myself included.

³ My greetings to Prisca and Aquila, my fellow workers in Christ Jesus, ⁴ ·who risked death to save my life: I am not the only one to owe them a debt of gratitude, all the churches among the pagans do as well. ⁵ ·My greetings also to the church that meets at their house.

⁶ Greetings to my friend Epaenetus, the first of Asia's gifts to Christ; greetings to Mary who ⁷ worked so hard for you; ·to those outstanding apostles Andronicus and Junias, my compatriots and fellow prisoners who became Christians before me; ⁸ ·to Ampliatus, my friend in ⁹ the Lord; ·to Urban, my fellow worker in ¹⁰ Christ; to my friend Stachys; ·to Apelles who has gone through so much for Christ; to everyone who belongs to the household of Aristobulus; ¹¹ ·to my compatriot Herodion; to those in the household of Narcissus who belong to ¹² the Lord; ·to Tryphaena and Tryphosa, who work hard for the Lord; to my friend Persis ¹³ who has done so much for the Lord; ·to Rufus, a chosen servant of the Lord, and to his mother ¹⁴ who has been a mother to me too. ·Greetings to Asyncritus, Phlegon, Hermes, Patrobas, Hermas, and all the brothers who are with

15 them; ·to Philologus and Julia, Nereus and his sister, and Olympas and all the saints who are
16 with them. ·Greet each other with a holy kiss. All the churches of Christ send greetings.

✠

The exact relationship of Romans 16 to the rest of this letter is in doubt. This passage appears to be an appendix, detachable from the first fifteen chapters that seemed to conclude with 15:33. The greetings and naming of people Paul seems to know very well personally (16:1–15) and the abrupt, strong warnings that follow in 16:17–20, which are at variance with the tone of the rest of the epistle, together with the repetitious character of the additional ending in 16:25–27, suggest that Romans 16 is a kind of afterthought that may not have originally been planned as part of Paul's communication with the Christians at Rome.

According to this theory, in the first fifteen chapters of Romans, Paul gave his gospel its most clear, objective development to date. Then, confident that this presentation could serve others, he decided to send it, together with a cover letter (i.e., 16:1–27), to others. He sent the letter that has come down to us with a messenger, Phoebe (16:1–2). Possibly these other recipients of Romans were Christians at Ephesus, where many of the friends whom Paul greets lived. Paul identifies one member of this community, Epaenetus, as "the first of Asia's gifts to Christ" (16:6), which suggests a community in Asia such as Ephesus. This theory explains the intimate character and personal knowledge of the community reflected in the warm greetings (16:3–16), the strong warnings (16:17–20) and the last greetings, together with a kind of postscript (16:21–27). These indicate a more involved, personal tone and distinguish Romans 16 from the rest of the epistle. And, of course, it also would explain the detachable character of this chapter and the fact that it follows an apparent conclusion in 15:33.

Further, this theory helps us to appreciate the more general appeal of Romans which might have been judged very early as appropriate for more than one community. It may also be noted that the phrase "in Rome" (1:7,15) could easily be deleted so that the message of the letter could serve as instruction and encouragement to any community. But to suggest that Romans 16 does not seem to have been an original part of Paul's letter to the church at Rome is not to say that this text has less importance. It is, for example, a particularly suggestive source of lively discussion about the place of women in Paul's life and in the life of the early church. In the list of twenty-five or so persons Paul names in 16:1–16, there are eight women and he refers to at least two others—i.e., Rufus' mother (16:13) and Nereus' sister (16:15). Thus, we are immediately struck by the relatively important role women played in the community Paul addressed—no small feat if they would have had to remain silent (1 Co 14:34–35) as they made their influence felt! In addition to their numbers, several of these women held positions of authority and responsibility in this church.

Phoebe, the first mentioned, may have been the

bearer of this cover letter (i.e., Romans 16), with a copy of 1:1–15:33 to the community of Ephesus. Paul does not send her greetings but tells his readers to welcome her (16:1–2). Phoebe is, Paul reminds them, a person of authority—a "deacon" who has influence over many, even Paul himself. Whether the title "deacon" referred to the specific office as described in Ac 6:1–7 (seven men appointed to distribute food to needy widows) or simply to the more general category of servants (i.e., the original meaning of "deacon") is not sure. In any case, two significant observations can be made. First, the reference in Rm 16:1 to Phoebe, a female deacon, contains the oldest and the first New Testament designation of this Christian service. Secondly, this woman has a position of authority recognized by Paul and the church and her sex was not a deterrent. In fact, it was not an issue.

The other persons named are also significant. Prisca (or Priscilla) is listed with her husband, Aquila (16:3–5). This Jewish-Christian couple had to flee Rome because of the edict which Emperor Claudius issued in A.D. 49, expelling all Jews from the city (cf. Ac 18:1–2). Paul met Prisca and Aquila in Corinth, and while it is possible that they had returned to Rome by the time this letter was written (Claudius died in A.D. 53 or 54), it is also possible that they settled elsewhere, for example, in Ephesus (cf. 1 Co 16:19). Paul greets "the church that meets at their house" (Rm 16:5), another example of the recognition the Apostle gives to the leadership of women in the early church (cf. Lydia's house-church, Ac 16:14–15,40).

Prisca and Aquila are called Paul's "fellow workers" (Rm 16:3). This designation (cf. 16:21; Ph 4:3; Phm 1, 24) is equivalent to "God's fellow workers" (cf. 1 Co 3:9; 1 Th 3:2), an indication that Paul does not imagine any other ministry of the gospel than one obedient and accountable directly to God. It is another man-woman team, Andronicus and Junias (possibly husband and wife, like Aquila and Prisca), whom Paul calls "outstanding apostles . . . compatriots and fellow prisoners" (Rm 16:7). Ancient manuscripts support the feminine reading "Junia." There are no existing parallels or inscriptions that suggest "Junias" as a man's name. This identification of a woman as an apostle is unique in the New Testament, which is probably why virtually all modern biblical translations have used a masculinized form, "Junias." Yet even the early church fathers (e.g., Origen, Jerome, John Chrysostom), hardly ardent feminists, took this to be a feminine name, "Junia," and commented on the honor it was for a woman to be named an apostle.

Paul tells the Christians to "greet each other with a holy kiss" (16:16). The ritual embrace that became characteristic of Christians when they gathered together at religious services signified the unity among them as they recognized each other as "saints." None of the usual divisions of social, economic or sexual inequality, Paul says, were to mar this unity (cf. 1 Co 11:17–20, 12:13; Ga 3:28; Col 3:11) which was celebrated in the liturgy. The "holy kiss" was to be a symbol for all Christians and for the world that Christ had overcome all barriers and differences between them.

STUDY QUESTIONS: How does the church recognize (or fail to recognize) the ministries of women today? Can it be legitimate in Christian practice to exclude certain people from ministry? What does this passage reveal about Paul's self-image as minister?

Romans 16:17-27
THE OBEDIENCE OF FAITH

¹⁷ I implore you, brothers, be on your guard against anybody who encourages trouble or puts difficulties in the way of the doctrine you ¹⁸ have been taught. Avoid them. ·People like that are not slaves of Jesus Christ, they are slaves of their own appetites, confusing the simple-minded with their pious and persuasive ¹⁹ arguments. ·Your fidelity to Christ, anyway, is famous everywhere, and that makes me very happy about you. I only hope that you are also wise in what is good and innocent of what is ²⁰ bad. ·The God of peace will soon crush Satan beneath your feet. The grace of our Lord Jesus Christ be with you.

²¹ Timothy, who is working with me, sends his greetings; so do my compatriots, Lucius, Jason ²² and Sosipater. ·I, Tertius, who wrote out this ²³ letter, greet you in the Lord. ·Greetings from Gaius, who is entertaining me and from the whole church that meets in his house. Erastus, the city treasurer, sends his greetings; so does our brother Quartus.

²⁵ Glory to him who is able to give you the strength to live according to the Good News I preach, and in which I proclaim Jesus Christ, the revelation of a mystery kept secret for end- ²⁶ less ages, ·but now so clear that it must be broadcast to pagans everywhere to bring them to the obedience of faith. This is only what scripture has predicted, and it is all part of the ²⁷ way the eternal God wants things to be. ·He

alone is wisdom; give glory therefore to him through Jesus Christ for ever and ever. Amen.

✠

Paul's warning against false teachers in 16:17–20 seems like an abrupt insert between the personal greetings to people Paul knew and greetings from people Paul is with. Its sharpness is also incongruent with the rest of the epistle and, because the threat seems to be fairly strong, it is surprising that Paul would so casually mention this danger tucked in as a kind of postscript. It would be more likely that Paul would speak adamantly in the body of the letter, warning against listening to falsehood, such as he did in Galatians (Ga 1:6–10, 5:10–12). This anomaly gives further support to the theory that this problem was not one which afflicted the Roman community to whom the main body of the letter was written, but was a reminder to the addressees designated in 16:1–27. It is possible that Paul's contact with these addressees (at Ephesus?) is so steady and communication between them so dependable that Paul finds it sufficient simply to add a word of encouragement regarding any divisive influence in their midst. Since they have many strong leaders whom he names and who can be depended upon, Paul simply reminds them to be vigilant. The admonition to be on guard (16:17) is a posture Jesus himself advocates for his followers (e.g., Lk 12:1). Paul's confidence in eventual victory is based on both the quality of good leadership and the hope that "soon"

God will end the struggle with Satan by crushing him (Rm 16:20). The expectation of the imminent moment when the conflict between God and Satan will be finished is never really far from Paul's mind apparently (cf., for example, 1 Co 7:29-31, 15:51-57; 2 Th 2:4-12). His preoccupation with this "time" is reflected also in Rm 13:11-14 where he says, "You must wake up now . . . Let your armor be the Lord Jesus Christ."

The allusion to the ritual embrace in 16:16 suggested a liturgical context as the original setting in which this letter was probably read. The doxology which brings the whole epistle to a close indicates such a context (16:25-27). In closing, Paul praises God for giving strength to the Christians which allows them to live the gospel. The content of Paul's proclamation is that God works for the fulfillment of the universal plan for salvation (16:26). This is what the scriptures predicted. This is the meaning of wisdom whereby God is given glory (16:27). The conclusion is actually very simple—the outcome of the gospel is the glory of God.

The style, vocabulary and even the use of a concluding hymn of praise as the end of a letter is somewhat foreign to Paul. Nevertheless, the main ideas themselves are Pauline. We have in 16:25-27, as a matter of fact, a little gem of a summary of some basic characteristics of Paul. While he may not often conclude whole letters like this, Paul does cap some of the most significant sections of his writings in this way (cf. 8:31-39, 11:33-36). And the Apostle is apt to express praise and confidence in the unfolding of the plan of God especially when confronted with a paradox such as he just considered, namely, a warm, appreciative description of his many co-workers and an acknowledgment that there are also false teachers troubling the community (16:17–20; cf. Ga 1:6–9). Paul sums up his thoughts with a call to give glory to God whose wishes have been revealed "through Jesus Christ" (Rm 16:27). The final "Amen" indicates Paul's faith that nothing happens which cannot become part of God's plan and resound to the glory of Jesus Christ.

STUDY QUESTIONS: Paul warns against false teachers, who, he says, are "slaves to their own appetites" (16:18). What could he mean by this? Can a minister or teacher seem to be more self-serving than God-serving? How? How does a person discern what is "good"? What is the role of "wisdom"? How is it acquired? How is Jesus Christ a "revelation of a mystery kept secret for endless ages" (16:25)? What is this mystery?

SUGGESTED FURTHER READINGS

Betz, H. D. *Galatians*. Hermeneia Commentaries. Philadelphia: Fortress Press, 1979. Probably the best classic-style, scholarly, recent commentary on Galatians in English. Written by a renowned Pauline scholar.

Bruce, F. F. *Paul: Apostle of the Heart Set Free*. Grand Rapids, Mich.: Eerdmans, 1977. Packed with information, insights and wisdom which help Paul come alive for the reader. Essential for a student of the life and writings of Paul.

Donfried, K. P., ed. *The Romans Debate*. Minneapolis: Augsburg, 1977. A collection of essays contributing to the debate on Paul's purposes for writing this most significant epistle.

Hooker, Morna D. *A Preface to Paul*. New York: Oxford University Press, 1980. Six articles on central issues in Paul's writings. A good introduction.

Käsemann, Ernst. *Commentary on Romans*. Trans. and ed. by Geoffrey W. Bromiley. Grand Rapids, Mich.: Eerdmans, 1980. A significant commentary by an important German scholar.

Maly, Eugene. *Romans*. New Testament Message 9. Wilmington, Del.: Michael Glazier, 1980. A final testament to Maly's lifelong exegetical and pastoral synthesis of Paul.

Osiek, Carolyn. *Galatians*. New Testament Message 12. Wilmington, Del.: Michael Glazier, 1980. Eminently readable and understandable interpretation of Paul's letter to the Galatians.

Robinson, J. A. T. *Wrestling with Romans*. Philadelphia: Westminster Press, 1979. An innovative, essay-type commentary by this controversial author. Engaging style.

Stendahl, Krister. *Paul Among Jews and Gentiles*. Philadelphia: Fortress Press, 1976. In this volume, Stendahl republishes important essays which provide a critique of some traditional interpretations in favor of identifying Paul's own theology and experience. An enlightening, challenging collection.

Taylor, Michael J., ed. *A Companion to Paul: Readings in Pauline Theology*. New York: Alba House, 1975. A collection of significant background articles contributed by well-known American and European Pauline scholars.

OTHER IMAGE BOOKS

AGING: THE FULFILLMENT OF LIFE – Henri J. M. Nouwen and Walter J. Gaffney
APOLOGIA PRO VITA SUA – John Henry Cardinal Newman
AN AQUINAS READER – Ed., with an Intro., by Mary T. Clark
BATTLE FOR THE AMERICAN CHURCH – Msgr. George A. Kelly
BIRTH OF THE MESSIAH – Raymond E. Brown
BREAKTHROUGH: MEISTER ECKHART'S CREATION SPIRITUALITY IN NEW TRANSLATION – Matthew Fox
CATHOLIC AMERICA – John Cogley
CATHOLIC PENTECOSTALISM – Rene Laurentin
CHRISTIAN LIFE PATTERNS – Evelyn and James Whitehead
THE CHURCH – Hans Küng
CITY OF GOD – St. Augustine – Ed. by Vernon J. Bourke. Intro. by Étienne Gilson
A CONCISE HISTORY OF THE CATHOLIC CHURCH (Revised Edition) – Thomas Bokenkotter
THE CONFESSIONS OF ST. AUGUSTINE – Trans., with an Intro., by John K. Ryan
CONJECTURES OF A GUILTY BYSTANDER – Thomas Merton
CONTEMPLATION IN A WORLD OF ACTION – Thomas Merton
CONTEMPLATIVE PRAYER – Thomas Merton
CREATIVE MINISTRY – Henri J. M. Nouwen
DARK NIGHT OF THE SOUL – St. John of the Cross. Ed. and trans. by E. Allison Peers
EVERLASTING MAN – G. K. Chesterton
THE FOUR GOSPELS: AN INTRODUCTION (Vol. 1) – Bruce Vawter, C.M.
THE FREEDOM OF SEXUAL LOVE – Joseph and Lois Bird
GENESEE DIARY – Henri J. M. Nouwen
HANS KÜNG: HIS WORK AND HIS WAY – Hermann Häring and Karl-Josef Kuschel
HAS SIN CHANGED? – Seán Fagan
A HISTORY OF PHILOSOPHY: VOLUME 1 – GREECE AND ROME (2 Parts) – Frederick Copleston, S.J.
A HISTORY OF PHILOSOPHY: VOLUME 2 – MEDIAEVAL PHILOSOPHY (2 Parts) – Frederick Copleston, S.J. Part I – Augustine to Bonaventure. Part II – Albert the Great to Duns Scotus
A HISTORY OF PHILOSOPHY: VOLUME 3 – LATE MEDIAEVAL AND RENAISSANCE PHILOSOPHY (2 Parts) – Frederick Copleston, S.J. Part I – Ockham to the Speculative Mystics. Part II – The Revival of Platonism to Suárez

OTHER IMAGE BOOKS

A HISTORY OF PHILOSOPHY: VOLUME 4 – MODERN PHILOSOPHY: Descartes to Leibniz – Frederick Copleston, S.J.

A HISTORY OF PHILOSOPHY: VOLUME 5 – MODERN PHILOSOPHY: The British Philosophers, Hobbes to Hume (2 Parts) – Frederick Copleston, S.J. Part I – Hobbes to Paley. Part II – Berkeley to Hume

A HISTORY OF PHILOSOPHY: VOLUME 6 – MODERN PHILOSOPHY (2 Parts) – Frederick Copleston, S.J. – The French Enlightenment to Kant

A HISTORY OF PHILOSOPHY: VOLUME 7 – MODERN PHILOSOPHY (2 Parts) – Frederick Copleston, S.J. Part I – Fichte to Hegel. Part II – Schopenhauer to Nietzsche

A HISTORY OF PHILOSOPHY: VOLUME 8 – MODERN PHILOSOPHY: Bentham to Russell (2 Parts) – Frederick Copleston, S.J. Part I – British Empiricism and the Idealist Movement in Great Britain. Part II – Idealism in America, the Pragmatist Movement, the Revolt against Idealism

A HISTORY OF PHILOSOPHY: VOLUME 9 – Maine de Biran to Sartre (2 Parts) – Frederick Copleston, S.J. Part I – The Revolution to Henri Bergson. Part II – Bergson to Sartre

THE IMITATION OF CHRIST – Thomas à Kempis. Ed., with Intro., by Harold C. Gardiner, S.J.

INVITATION TO ACTS – Robert J. Karris

INVITATION TO THE BOOK OF REVELATION – Elisabeth Schüssler Fiorenza

INVITATION TO JOHN – George MacRae

INVITATION TO LUKE – Robert J. Karris

INVITATION TO MARK – Paul J. Achtemeier

INVITATION TO MATTHEW – Donald Senior

INVITATION TO THE NEW TESTAMENT EPISTLES I – Mary Ann Getty

INVITATION TO THE NEW TESTAMENT EPISTLES II – Eugene A. LaVerdiere

INVITATION TO THE NEW TESTAMENT EPISTLES III – Luke Timothy Johnson

INVITATION TO THE NEW TESTAMENT EPISTLES IV – Frederick W. Danker

THE JESUS MYTH – Andrew M. Greeley

JOURNAL OF A SOUL – Pope John XXIII

THE JOY OF BEING HUMAN – Eugene Kennedy

KEY TO THE BIBLE – Wilfrid J. Harrington, O.P.

OTHER IMAGE BOOKS

Vol. 1 – The Record of Revelation
Vol. 2 – The Old Testament: Record of the Promise
Vol. 3 – The New Testament: Record of the Fulfillment
KÜNG IN CONFLICT – Leonard Swidler
LIFE AND HOLINESS – Thomas Merton
LIFE IS WORTH LIVING – Fulton J. Sheen
THE LIFE OF ALL LIVING – Fulton J. Sheen
LIFE OF CHRIST – Fulton J. Sheen
LILIES OF THE FIELD – William E. Barrett
LITTLE FLOWERS OF ST. FRANCIS – Trans. by Raphael Brown
LIVING IN HOPE – Ladislaus Boros, S.J.
LOVE IS ALL – Joseph and Lois Bird
MAN WITH A SONG – Francis and Helen Line
MARRIAGE IS FOR GROWNUPS – Joseph and Lois Bird
MODELS OF THE CHURCH – Avery Dulles
THE MONASTIC JOURNEY – Thomas Merton
THE NEW SEXUALITY: MYTHS, FABLES AND HANG-UPS – Eugene C. Kennedy
THE NEW TESTAMENT OF THE JERUSALEM BIBLE: Reader's Edition – Alexander Jones, General Editor
THE NEW TESTAMENT OF THE NEW AMERICAN BIBLE (complete and unabridged)
THE OLD TESTAMENT OF THE JERUSALEM BIBLE: Reader's Edition – Alexander Jones, General Editor
Volume 2: 1 Samuel – 2 Maccabees; Volume 3: Job – Ecclesiasticus; Volume 4: The Prophets – Malachi
THE OLD TESTAMENT WITHOUT ILLUSION – John L. McKenzie
ORTHODOXY – G. K. Chesterton
THE PAIN OF BEING HUMAN – Eugene Kennedy
POWER TO THE PARENTS! – Joseph and Lois Bird
THE PSALMS OF THE JERUSALEM BIBLE – Alexander Jones, General Editor
A RELIGIOUS HISTORY OF THE AMERICAN PEOPLE (2 vols.) – Sydney E. Ahlstrom
RENEWING THE EARTH – Ed. by David J. O'Brien and Thomas A. Shannon
THE ROMAN CATHOLIC CHURCH – John L. McKenzie
ST. FRANCIS OF ASSISI – G. K. Chesterton
ST. FRANCIS OF ASSISI – Johannes Jorgensen
SAINT THOMAS AQUINAS – G. K. Chesterton
SAINTS FOR ALL SEASONS – John J. Delaney, editor

OTHER IMAGE BOOKS

THE SCREWTAPE LETTERS (Illus.) – C. S. Lewis
THE SEXUAL CELIBATE – Donald Goergen
THE SHROUD OF TURIN (Revised Edition) – Ian Wilson
THE SINAI MYTH – Andrew M. Greeley
THE SPIRIT OF CATHOLICISM – Karl Adam
SPIRITUAL CANTICLE – St. John of the Cross. Trans. and ed., with an Intro., by E. Allison Peers
THE SPIRITUAL EXERCISES OF ST. IGNATIUS – Trans. by Anthony Mottola, Ph.D. Intro. by Robert W. Gleason, S.J.
THE STORY OF THE TRAPP FAMILY SINGERS – Maria Augusta Trapp
SUFFERING – Louis Evely
SUMMA THEOLOGIAE – Thomas Aquinas. General Editor: Thomas Gilby, O.P.
  Volume 1: The Existence of God. Part One: Questions 1–13
A THEOLOGY OF THE OLD TESTAMENT – John L. McKenzie
THIRSTING FOR THE LORD/Essays in Biblical Spirituality – Carroll Stuhlmueller
THIS MAN JESUS – Bruce Vawter
THOMAS MERTON – Cornelia and Irving Sussman
A THOMAS MERTON READER – Revised Edition – Ed. by Thomas P. McDonnell
TOWARD A NEW CATHOLIC MORALITY – John Giles Milhaven
TREASURE IN CLAY – The Autobiography of Fulton J. Sheen
UNDERSTANDING MYSTICISM – Ed. by Richard Woods, O.P.
THE WIT AND WISDOM OF BISHOP FULTON J. SHEEN – Ed. by Bill Adler
WITH GOD IN RUSSIA – Walter J. Ciszek, S.J., with Daniel L. Flaherty, S.J.
THE WOUNDED HEALER – Henri J. M. Nouwen